Unlocked Treasures

Unlocked Treasures

Contemplative Aspects of Faith

JEFFREY D. JOHNSON

WIPF & STOCK · Eugene, Oregon

UNLOCKED TREASURES
Contemplative Aspects of Faith

Copyright © 2011 Jeffrey D. Johnson. All rights reserved. Except for brief quotations in critical publications or reviews, no part of this book may be reproduced in any manner without prior written permission from the publisher. Write: Permissions, Wipf and Stock Publishers, 199 W. 8th Ave., Suite 3, Eugene, OR 97401.

Wipf & Stock
An Imprint of Wipf and Stock Publishers
199 W. 8th Ave., Suite 3
Eugene, OR 97401
www.wipfandstock.com

ISBN 13: 978-1-61097-150-8

Manufactured in the U.S.A.

All scripture quotations are from: The New King James Version, Copyright 1982, by Thomas Nelson, Inc. unless otherwise noted.
Scripture taken from the HOLY BIBLE, NEW INTERNATIONAL VERSION. Copyright 1973, 1978, 1984 International Bible Society. Used by permission of Zondervan Bible Publishers.

Scripture taken from the Holy Bible, King James Version.

Dr. Jeffrey D. Johnson is the founder and president of Israel Today Ministries and is a conference speaker, teacher, pastor, religious writer, and humanitarian. He can be contacted at:

> Israel Today Ministries
> PO Box 150288
> Arlington, Texas 76015
> www.israeltodayministries.org,
> galileeman@juno.com

Jewish mystics say that in eternity past God created all the souls that would ever exist. He then divided them into two, male and female; therefore, each soul is only one half. The idea is that when a child is born they begin a journey with the objective of finding their other half, thus completing their soul. When they find their other half, they have found their "soul-mate."

My wife, Louise, is my soul-mate. She thoroughly completes all that I am or desire to be. She is the one who taught me to be contemplative, to see the nuance in life and faith.

Jeffrey D. Johnson
September 2010
143 (our secret)

Contents

1 **ADVENTURES IN THE HOLY LAND** 1
- a. A High Place
- b. Gentile! Yeah, You!
- c. Old Man with a Car
- d. On the Roof
- e. The Phone Call
- f. Tones of a Mother
- g. War and Peace

2 **BIBLICAL PRINCIPLES** 16
- a. Be of Good Cheer
- b. Being Blessed
- c. Body, Soul, Spirit
- d. Church Understood
- e. Drawing in Miracles
- f. Early Will I Seek You
- g. Enlarge Thy Tent
- h. I am Jesus
- i. Israel: "One Who Strives With God"
- j. Known in the Gates
- k. Life
- l. The Silent God
- m. Spirituality and Bible Study
- n. Spirituality and Prayer
- o. Spirituality and Worship
- p. The Hem of His Garment
- q. The Lord's Prayer
- r. Walking on Water
- s. What is Love?
- t. Who is Jesus?

3   **ENCOURAGEMENT** 52
   a. Being in Christ
   b. Change
   c. Community
   d. Do I Fear God?
   e. Don't Be Afraid
   f. God's Navel
   g. He made the Stars Also
   h. Importance of Life
   i. It Does Matter
   j. Music
   k. No Shortcuts
   l. Regarding Unanimity
   m. Yes, Jesus Loves Me!

4   **HEBRAIC THOUGHTS** 66
   a. The Scriptures Jesus Read and Origen, an Early Church Father
   b. Blessing
   c. Christian-ese
   d. Halakah: Walking the Walk
   e. Isaac Was Comforted
   f. Jesus and Hanukkah
   g. Light
   h. Mourning Lost Temples
   i. Perseverance Through Hard Times
   j. Mysteries: Tisha B'Av
   k. Our Debt: Part One
   l. Our Debt: Part Two
   m. Repentance – *Teshuvah*
   n. Seasons to Remember
   o. Shavuot: Feast of Pentecost
   p. It Began with a Sigh!
   q. The Seventh Month: Part One
   r. The Seventh Month: Part Two
   s. The Seventh Month: Part Three
   t. Times of the Gentiles
   u. Treasures in the Sand

5   LIST LESSONS   103
   a. God is Many Things
   b. Grace
   c. Significance
   d. Longing
   e. The Wonder of His Name

6   QUESTIONS FOR THE PASTOR   109
   a. Where Will We Dwell in Eternity?
   b. Resurrection of the Old Testament Saints
   c. Where Will the Baby or Child God After Death?

1

Adventures in the Holy Land

a. A HIGH PLACE

WALKING WITH A FRIEND on top of the mountain that overlooked the beautiful city of Haifa, we beheld the places where the *Nevi'im* (prophets) walked and brought light into a dark world. We came to a high place where there were 15–20 people gathered, mostly adults. They were quietly singing, reading Scripture, socializing, hugging, laughing, and basically enjoying one another's company.

Praying

They have gathered here in this same spot during the same hour on the same day for several years. Why? To pray! Yes, I said to pray. These are members of a small congregation. For years, members of the congregation have come on Wednesday evening to pray on this high place over looking their city below. They are praying for the souls of their community to come to a saving knowledge of the Holy One. They are praying that they may know the peace of God and the forgiveness of sins through Messiah Yeshua—Jesus Christ.

To say that I was moved is an understatement. How many congregations do we know that have a significant amount of members faithfully go to a special place on the same day and at the same hour for years to pray for the salvation of their community, neighbors, and friends?

Linked with Survival

Maybe it is because they are in a war zone—perhaps. Most members of this congregation have very little, and yet out of their poverty they give all they have. They cry over lost loved ones, rejoice when others rejoice, sorrow when others sorrow. A great sense of community is linked with survival among believers in most of the world. It is good for us to pray, weep, and rejoice with one another.

"Those who sow in tears shall reap in joy. He who continually goes forth weeping, bearing seed for sowing, shall doubtless come again, with rejoicing, bringing his sheaves with him."

—PSALM 126:5–6

b. GENTILE! YEAH, YOU!
Finally Met

I sat in the humble, low-ceilinged, cramped office of a local Jewish pastor. It was a special blessing because we knew people who knew people and our paths had crisscrossed along the way and now we finally met.

He and his wife made *aliyah* (moving to Israel) around 20 years ago. God led him to start a Bible study group in Northern Israel—a Bible study which has become a growing congregation. We chatted about theology, the challenges that face believers today, and the special needs in Israel.

It is humbling to have the opportunity to encourage leaders here in Israel. There is such a great need for training, humanitarian relief, and tools for ministry. We are so blessed in the States. We have everything we need at our fingertips. Not so in this part of the world.

Help of Gentiles

He implied, "We could not do this without your help, the help of Gentile believers," quoting Isaiah 60. We talked about how we work together blessing the seed of Abraham. It is true! God said that the Gentile will bless Zion in the context of the last days. Let's take a brief look.

The context of Isaiah 60 is the Millennial Kingdom, the rule and reign of Messiah for one thousand years.

Verses 1–3: Light shines in the darkness and the nations shall come to the Light which is the glory of the Lord. The Lord Jesus establishes his kingdom rule. Finally, the Messianic era of peace begins.

Verses 4–13: Treasures from all around the world shall come to Israel during the Kingdom age. There will be so much treasure from the nations that the gates will remain open continually.

Verses 14–18: Those who afflicted Israel will bow before them. There will be peace and calm—quite the contrast of the violence described in Israel 59:6–8.

Verses 19–22: God blesses Israel immeasurably. "The Lord will hasten it in its time."

Fulfillment of Prophecy

One striking point that the Gentile believer should understand is this: "The sons of foreigners shall build up your walls" (verse 10). Foreigners are the Gentiles. Building up walls is a reference of blessing, safety and provision. In the last days, the Gentile will aid Israel. During the Millennial Kingdom of Messiah, this will unfold in profound ways. In the general context of latter years, it would apply to Gentiles (particularly those who believe in Jesus) who will come to Israel's side.

c. OLD MAN WITH A CAR

90 Degrees

Much of the West Bank is poor and underdeveloped, yet you will find pockets of wealthy neighborhoods and a middle class. Walking at midday, with the temperature around 90 plus degrees, I asked an elderly Arab man for directions to my destination. He walked me to the corner and pointed in a direction. We exchanged nice words and I went on my way.

Beeping

About ten minutes into my journey—which, by the way, was uphill—I heard a car and beeping behind me. I turned and saw that it was the old man and a teenage boy. He was in a very old, beat-up car. The glove compartment door wouldn't shut and black smoke exhaust was pouring out the back. The tires were bald and the lining of the roof was falling down. The belts screeched as he pressed the gas pedal.

Get In

He said, "Get in! This is my son. We will take you to where you want to go. It is a hot day!" I got in the car, which I greatly welcomed as a chance to sit and be driven up the big hill, rather than walking. It was like receiving a cup of cold water.

The old man started to talk. He said, "I am a Christian Catholic. My name is Joseph, and this is my son, Christopher. We will help you find your place." We had a delightful conversation.

When we arrived at my destination, we shook hands and I said, "Thank you very much. God bless you." I shook his son's hand, who had graciously climbed into the back seat so I could sit with his father.

Turn It Around

You say, "Okay, Dr. Jeff, nice story. So what?" Let's turn the story around. A stranger walks up to you. He is hot, sweaty, a little stinky around the edges, has a different color skin, a different accent, different clothing, and asks for directions. You tell him how to go to his destination. The stranger leaves and goes on his way.

Now, you had plans for the day. God tells you to help this stranger, to take you son and teach him how to do a good thing for a stranger. So, you get in your run-down, beat-up car, not having money for gas, and you go and find the stranger, pick him up, honor him, talk with him, witness to him, and take him to his destination. That is what this Christian Catholic did for me that day.

"And whoever gives one of these little ones only a cup of cold water in the name of a disciple, assuredly, I say to you, he shall by no means lose his reward."

—MATTHEW 10:42

They Never Forget

What this man did for me that day is just like what we all are supposed to do: Give, as it were, temporary relief—a cup of cold water, a meal, a little hope, a little encouragement—perhaps just enough to give people the resources to reach their destination.

They will never forget you who came in the name of Jesus to bless them at their time of need. They will never forget that this blessing came from loving Christians who had other plans but who gave generously of their time and resources.

Do the right thing.

d. ON THE ROOF

On Saint Mark Street in the Old City is an old metal stairway that curiously leads to the roof of an ancient building. To find this place, one must meander through the aged stoned paved streets, and off to the left—you may miss it—you'll find this iron ladder ascending upward. Climbing up, you begin to discover that it is more than an ascent to a roof; rather, you are now atop the roofs of a large section covering the Jewish and Arab quarters.

We found people praying, having a lunch with friends, police, Jews and Arabs walking and seemingly being reflective as to the view. We could see the Mount of Olives and the Temple Mount area. Church steeples and bell towers stood majestically overlooking the Christian quarter, minarets dotted the Muslim section, and we beheld the beautiful buildings of the Jewish quarter. What a vista!

Part of the connecting roofs was flat, some were rounded, and a few had small walls dividing property. In one section, there was a horizontal metal grate which looked like a chimney, and looking down you could see people walking through the streets below. These roofs were literally over the streets and alleyways as well as houses and shops.

It is never peaceful for very long in the Middle East before something happens. Sure enough, while Louise and I were taking in this serene, spiritual experience on the rooftops, a woman with a frightened look on her face came swiftly towards us. She said frantically, "Will you help me? This man is following me!" Here we go . . .

There he was. I assured the woman I'd take care of it. I blocked his path, and though he could not speak English and I could not speak Arabic, I told him to back off and leave. We argued and eventually he did leave. We stood there and watched to be sure that he did leave. He climbed down the stairway and faded into the press of people in the streets below. Louise and I comforted the woman and directed her to a safe section in the Old City. Whew! Confronting this man was the longest 90 seconds of our trek that day. God protected us, and we are most grateful. Your prayers do count—keep on!

There is a history of being up on a roof in Scripture. Today, like thousands of years ago, people use the top of their home for various reasons. Rahab, who was on the threshold of watching her city be destroyed, used her home for a very important reason. Let's take a few moments and look at this marvelous and mysterious woman named Rahab.

Mystery of Rahab

Israel mourned the death of Moses for 30 days (until the 7th of Nissan, just a few days before Passover), during which time Joshua ordered two spies to cross the river for reconnaissance (Josh. 2:1). Rahab—who converted to the God of Abraham, Isaac, and Jacob—helped the spies and ultimately Israel in conquering Jericho, and, according to Jewish tradition, became the wife Joshua (Josh. 2–6).

Broad Space

Rahab, whose name means "broad space"—or better, "pride"—reminds us of one who lives in a worldly way, walking the broad path and full of pride. After hearing of the truth of God, she repented, believed, and was humbled, thus beginning her walk in the narrow path of life with God (Matt. 7:13, 14).

This woman became the ancestor of prophets and kings. She is an ancestor of Jesus (mother of Boaz, the husband of Ruth, and the great-grandmother of David). She is described as an example of living by faith (Heb. 11:31; Matt. 1:5; Ruth 4:18–21).

Culture

Rahab was an innkeeper who provided food. Some argue she was a prostitute. Either way, she was worldly by virtue of her culture and then became a believer.

Planks of Wood

The ruins of Jericho suggest that it was a relatively small city. However, the city was surrounded by two walls approximately 15 feet apart. Stone arches and planks of wood would have spanned the two walls. Houses would have been built upon this foundation. Today, in the Old City of Jerusalem, you will find many people still live atop shops, over alleyways, and near the wall. Rahab lived in such a house.

Scarlet

She hid the spies on top of her flat roof where they also slept that night. Making a deal with the spies, Rahab tied a scarlet cord in her window. When the Hebrew soldiers would come and see the scarlet cord, they would not harm anyone in the house.

The scarlet cord is identified in Jewish tradition with the scarlet thread used to mark the elder of Tamar's twin sons, Zerah (Gen. 38:28). Zerah, or Zerach, is the great-grandfather of Achan, who would trouble Israel in Joshua chapter seven. He is also mentioned in Matthew's genealogy of the Messiah (Mat. 1:3). Today, Jewish mystics following Kabbalah will wear a scarlet string around their wrist.

In Christian tradition, the scarlet cord reminds us of families that were spared at Passover by painting the blood around their doors. Also, the scarlet cord flowing from the window points to the blood of Christ. It is through the blood that we find cleansing, forgiveness, and eternal life.

40,000 Soldiers

When the 40,000-plus soldiers went up to Jericho, the foreign tribes began to tremble (Josh. 4:13, 5:1). Rahab and her family were nestled in her house with the scarlet cord flowing from her window. The rumbling, shouting, screaming, earth trembling, walls collapsing, swords clanging, arrows flying, spears being flung, shields being dented, blood flowing, and death everywhere would describe this horrible scene. Yet within her house, the people were safe.

Still Standing

Obviously, after the battle, the house was still standing atop the two walls, which suggests the walls fell everywhere except this one place. Rahab's house with the scarlet cord would have looked somewhat like a tower standing alone. With carnage all around, the remains of her house would have reminded the Israelites of Passover as the Egyptians experienced death and destruction while there was safety for those who believed in the protection of the blood (Ex. 12).

Perhaps the tower of Rahab's house would have reminded the Jews of the banner Moses erected long ago, a beacon of hope (Numbers 21:8–9).

Most assuredly, it reminds the Christian, the believer, of the cross, where Jesus hung between heaven and earth. All who look and believe will live.

Veiled Glory

Rahab's window also reminds us of another mysterious truth. A window illuminates a house, and yet not all of it. This is also true of the incarnation. Messiah Jesus hid his complete splendor and glory from the world, being veiled in flesh, only revealing enough divinity so that we may understand, confirming who he was through the death (the scarlet cord), burial, and resurrection. One day, his complete glory and splendor will be revealed when he returns.

Nestle In

The story of Joshua, Rahab, and Jericho is replete with messianic types and shadows. For now, our reflection is upon this woman who found refuge and redemption in the God of Abraham. She heard, she saw, and she believed and was changed forever (Josh. 6:22–23).

Among the rubble of this world, when hope seems depleted, there is a place you can go to find rest, refreshment, refuge, and redemption. Simply look for the scarlet cord, look to the beacon of hope on Calvary—Messiah Jesus, our Passover—and nestle in.

e. THE PHONE CALL

The streets were busy with the usual press of people selling their wares. It was afternoon, as my colleague and I were traveling in Jerusalem, when I received the phone call from one of my sons. Hearing your son's voice when you are in Israel and he is in another country within the Middle East is initially startling.

This time he was in Jordan, which is a friendlier, pro-western Arab country in the region. Oftentimes, he is in another country nearby that is not so pro-western. Nevertheless, while in Jordan, he was assisting a local congregation with some projects in a very poor section of the capital city, Amman. During this time, he became acquainted with a large Muslim family, a family of renown within their community. This dear family had shown my son gracious hospitality.

The head of the home is a distinguished, gray-haired businessman who is well respected in Amman. He has four sons and five daughters. He and his lovely wife are kind people living in a beautiful home within the upside of town.

Who is Your Father?

During this time, my son was living in a lowly apartment near the projects of the poorest section of the capital city. However, this Muslim family invited my son to stay a few days. One of their daughters is a believer in Jesus, which made the conversations very interesting. The father continued to ask my beloved son about his family. "Who is your father and what does he do?" "Where does your family live and where do they go?"

Family and reputation are very important in the Middle East. You are known by what you do and not so much by the words you speak. Though your words are very important, your actions speak volumes as to your character—thus, the reason for the phone call from my son.

"Dad, can you come to Jordan and validate who I am?" he asked. I understood his request and the meaning behind it, and I responded, "I will be there as soon as I can."

Our Plan

My colleague and I began making arrangements and preparations for our journey from Jerusalem to Amman. Our plan was to hire a driver to take us across into Jordan over the Hussein Bridge and checkpoint, which is up north, east of Beit She'an and south of the Galilee. The idea was to travel through the mountains in Jordan and then down to Amman. Our return plan was to go south to the Allenby Bridge and checkpoint near Jericho, reenter Israel, and be picked up by our dear friend Ramone. You may remember Ramone. He is the one who keeps me out of trouble and safe in the Middle East as I travel to and fro. It was a simple plan and it should work—and it did, for the most part without any mishaps.

After several hours driving through the hot dessert sun and cooling down somewhat as we were traveling through the mountains, we finally arrived in Amman. What a joy to see my son, who I hadn't seen in many months. He had lost a little weight, his skin looked a little weathered, and he had sharpness in his eyes like that of an eagle. The Middle East has a way of affecting people that way. My baby boy was no longer a baby boy; rather, he became a man somewhere along the journey.

We had refreshments and then went on our way to be introduced to the family. What an exercise in faith riding along in a car when someone else is driving through the streets of Amman! Organized chaos is the best way to describe the traffic. To say we were glad to get off the main road would be an understatement.

The Church

We first stopped by the church where he was helping in some of the projects. We met the pastor and his lovely wife and several of the children who were part of this tiny congregation. My heart always breaks for the children who are the ones who suffer the most in any military conflict or social economic crisis. My son was brilliant, loving, and with great compassion reflecting the love of Jesus to the people of this poor community in Jordan.

Meeting the Father

Next, we traveled through the winding streets with alleyways, leaving the trash-filled streets with burning barrels of fire to a more pristine part of town. We pulled up on a nice driveway and there before us was a beautiful home with a patio veranda around back. My son introduced me and my colleague to the father first and then to the rest of the family.

Introductions

I found it interesting when my son introduced me and my friend (oh, by the way, I never mentioned that my colleague is a Bible teacher in a Christian high school), for the response was "Ohhh!" or "Hmm!" I asked my son, "What did you say to them?" He said, "Dad I introduced you as a 'holy man' because you are a minister, and I introduced Chuck (my colleague) as 'one who studies holy books' because he is a Christian school teacher."

My son was now validated! He is known in that family and community as "Scott, son of the holy man Jeff."

That evening, the men sat in one part of the house and the daughters served their father, the "holy man," and "the one who studies holy books." Then came time for the photo. The father sat on a chair, I sat on one side, Chuck sat on the other, and the rest of the family and friends stood behind the patriarch and the honored guests.

My son now has an open door to return to this family. The father, by his actions and the words that he spoke, honored me by welcoming me into his home any time. His actions matched his words.

My Son's Sanctuary

With the mission accomplished, it was time for Chuck and me to travel back home to Israel. Before heading back to Israel, we had to sleep, as it was late in the evening. We stayed in my son's apartment. Walking through dark narrow streets, with dogs barking and cats meowing, passing trash cans, walking through the metal gate, up the stone stairs in the yard of dirt, to a stone building with bars across the windows with the smell of cat urine, we stepped across the threshold into this sanctuary of safety, peace, and love. We showered and cleaned up from our day. Sitting upon mattresses on the floor with a dim light bulb hanging from a wire overhead, the three of us prayed, read scripture, and thanked the Lord for a marvelous day. In the distance, you could hear the Muslim clerics sing their prayers, their voices echoing through the valleys.

As our heads hit our moldy pillows, our eyes closed and we went fast to sleep. Roosters and sounds of cats in the garbage woke us the next morning. It was time to travel back, literally crossing the Jordan River into the land of Abraham, Isaac, and Jacob.

Saying Goodbye

We said our goodbyes. Leaving your children is never an easy thing to do. My eyes filled with tears as our driver started his car and Chuck and I climbed in and down the road we went.

Finally, we came to the Allenby Bridge and the checkpoint near Jericho. Everything went fine until I discovered that my bag was stolen. We made it through the checkpoint and were now on the Israeli side. Still no bag. It was obviously stolen on the Jordanian side of security. It was my own foolish mistake. Usually, I keep my bag with me, but for some reason (we were pretty exhausted), I let it go through security without it being attached to my right arm.

"Follow us!"

I approached several Israeli soldiers and shared my plight with them. With swiftness and determination, they said, "Follow us!" I did. They escorted me back over to the Jordanian side of the checkpoint and we walked into the inner most part of Jordanian security, looking for my bag. It was like the parting of the Red Sea. The Jordanian security moved aside as they saw this six-foot-two American and a band of Israeli soldiers. It was quite impressive and intimidating at the same time.

We didn't find the bag. It was long gone. Lesson learned—hold on to your bags!

Loyal Friend

The whole process took about three hours. Meanwhile, Ramone, our dear friend who was to pick us up, stood outside by his car in the 115-degree heat of the Judean wilderness. We told him we would be there at a certain time. The time had come and gone. He was aggressively inquiring as to our safety and whereabouts. He was running out of water, and yet he stayed there until we came through the gates of the checkpoint.

Ramone is the type of man that would have waited for us throughout the night. Why? Because we said we would be there, and as friends, we have proven that our words match our actions. We have blessed his family and he has blessed ours.

When we finally walked through the gates and saw his dehydrated body standing near the car, we were delighted, to say the least. His arms were waving and he was shouting, "*Baruch HaShem!*" ("Praise the Lord!") He said over and over, "Praise the Lord, you are all right, my brother!" We hugged his sweat-soaked body, he kissed us on the cheeks, and we piled into the car. Up to Jerusalem we would go. What a joy it was to be back home, driving up the Judean mountains, through the Mount of Olives and Mount Zion, finally arriving at Moriah, the main mountain of Jerusalem.

Principles to Remember

1. A father will respond to his son's request. So it is that our Heavenly Father will respond to his children when they call to him (Matthew 7:7–11).

2. What you do is who you are. You can say good words, and good words are necessary; however, it is your actions that measure you. You are known by what you do. (Proverbs 22:1; James 1:21–27, 2:14–20).

3. With friendship, loyalty is important. A true friend will lay down his life for another. Believers have a true friend that is closer than a brother (John 15:13–14; Proverbs 18:24).

4. There is joy in coming home. No matter how far you've traveled, there is joy in coming home. There is peace, love, acceptance, and assurance. For the believer, our home is found in Yeshua, the Messiah. Daily, you can walk with him and talk with him. Where Jesus is, there you will find the Christian's home. One day, we will rule and reign with Jesus for 1,000 years, where his throne will be in Jerusalem. We will also spend eternity with him throughout the ages to come. Those who believe in Jesus truly do find purpose and peace (Deuteronomy 28:13; Isaiah 2; Ezekiel 40–48; Matthew 25; John 14; Colossians 1; Revelation 20–22).

f. TONES OF A MOTHER

The crescent moon glistened high above the Mediterranean Sea as a warship patrolled the coastline, and within earshot I heard the tender tones of a mother telling the story of her days as a youth to her teenage daughter. The mother ended up chatting with me, explaining her conversation.

She grew up in the area upon the mountain of the prophet and was passing on the heritage of her youth to her daughter. A few moments later, an elderly woman with the scars of time written on her face and eyes that narrowed with wisdom and experience appeared. She was the grandmother. The grandmother chimed in on the conversation, admitting she was always pleased that her daughter played on these steep foothills of the mountain, and recalling how beautiful it was back then without the highways, houses, and press of people. She told me that her father moved to the area in 1929. The wide-eyed teenage granddaughter was smiling with pride, listening to her mother and grandmother speaking of the rich heritage she was learning.

Passing It Forward

I thought how appropriate it was to teach about heritage, history, and tradition on this day. You see, today is Shavuot, or Pentecost. The holiday is celebrated this year on June 8, 9, and 10. This was the day Moses received the Word of God from Mount Sinai. It is considered the birthday of Judaism. It is also the day the Holy Spirit descended upon those in the upper room, thus birthing the Church (Acts 2).

Shavuot, or the Feast of Pentecost, is one of the seven feasts described in Leviticus 23. Originally, Shavuot was an agricultural feast. Historically, the Jews would celebrate by reading the Books of Exodus, focusing on the receiving of the Law, and the Book of Ruth because of her devotion to the Law of God. Today, this tradition is still in vogue. Thousands in Jerusalem, after studying the Scriptures all night, will trek to the Western Wall, and as the sun rises they will recite a morning liturgical prayer. It is an amazing holiday to experience. Within the Messianic community, you will find great celebration during Shabbat services with teaching, preaching, dancing, singing, and animated expressions of joy.

I thought how wonderful it was for this mother and grandmother to rehearse their heritage with the younger generation, teaching her to remember why they believe what they believe and why they live they way that they live (Deut. 6:3–9).

Tell It Over and Over Again

The Church has a phenomenal story and history, beginning on the Day of Shavuot, tracing its history from the Law of Moses to the Spirit of God, giving life to those who believe in the God of Abraham, Isaac, and Jacob, trusting in the Messiah of Israel, Jesus of Nazareth, for redemption through his shed blood on Calvary.

It is bigger than a denominational bent or a political preference or a national DNA. The story of redemption goes back millennia—God's love for man has been demonstrated over and over again, ultimately culminating in the death, burial, and resurrection of Jesus Christ.

May believers in God's Messiah tell their children and children's children about their heritage that comes from God. Keep the tradition of Shavuot alive and tell the story of God's love and provision over and over again.

g. WAR AND PEACE

Israel braced for war with up to five enemies in the summer of 2007. According to WorldTribune.com, June 28, 2007, Israeli military intelligence had projected that a major attack could come from any of five adversaries: Iran, Syria, and/or their non-state clients (Hezbollah, Hamas, and Al Qaida). Maj. Gen. Amos Yadlin told the Cabinet that the Jewish state faced five adversaries in what could result in an imminent confrontation. "Each of these adversaries is capable of sparking a war in the summer," Yadlin was quoted as saying. Nothing has changed today.

The key to understanding what God is doing in the world, is to understand what God is doing in the Middle East, specifically Israel, more specifically Jerusalem.

It is ironic that Syria, the place where followers of Jesus were first called "Christians" (Acts 11:26); Gaza, where Philip preached the gospel to the Ethiopian eunuch, which probably resulted in Christianity being birthed in Ethiopia (Acts 8:26); and Iran, where King Cyrus, blessed Israel by allowing the Jews to go up to Jerusalem and rebuild the Temple (2 Chron. 36:23), are the same places that are giving modern-day Israel grief.

"Pray for the peace of Jerusalem."

—Ps. 122:6

2

Biblical Principles

a. BE OF GOOD CHEER!

THE APOSTLE PAUL, FACING a major threat on his life from some of the people in Jerusalem, was thrown into a dungeon, beaten and whipped by soldiers. Being a Christian does not guarantee a life without trials and testing along the way. In fact, if you are faithfully serving the Lord, you will probably face a multitude of trials. These are brought into your life to mold you into the image of Christ.

When the turbulent waves come, remember God's Word: "Fear not, for I have redeemed you; I have called you by name; you are mine. When you pass through the waters, I will be with you; and through the rivers, they shall not overflow you. When you walk through the fire, you shall not be burned; nor shall the flame scorch you" (Isaiah 43:1–2).

Shadrach, Meshach, and Abednego, facing the wrath of King Nebuchadnezzar because they would not bow down to worldly compromise, said this about the prospect of being thrown into the blazing furnace: "Our God whom we serve is able to deliver us from the burning fiery furnace, and He will deliver us from your hand, O king. But if not, let it be known to you, O king, that we do not serve your gods, nor will we worship the gold image which you have set up" (Daniel 3:17–18).

Ol' Nebuchadnezzar threw those three young men into the furnace and peeked in to watch them burn—and what he saw blew him away. He said, "Look! I see four men (not three, but four men) walking in the fire, and the form of the fourth is like the Son of God" (Dan. 3:25).

Jesus was with them! Listen: Christ is with his children all the time—especially with those who are faithfully and lovingly serving him. As we follow Christ, He is with us and will never leave us.

While chained in that dungeon, Paul's heart must have soared with renewed power and hope as Christ said to him, "Be of good cheer, Paul;

for as you have testified for Me in Jerusalem, so you must also bear witness at Rome" (Acts 23:11).

"Be of good cheer" is translated from one Greek word *tharseo*, which means "take courage; do not be afraid." It is a word that only Christ uses in the New Testament.

He used it five times, and each time he brought wonderful comfort.

1. He said to the paralytic, "Be of good cheer . . . Your sins are forgiven" (Mat. 9:2).
2. He said to the woman with the twelve-year hemorrhage, "Be of good cheer, your faith has made you well" (Mat. 9:22).
3. To his frightened disciples in the midst of the Sea of Galilee, as he walked on the water and approached the sinking boat, he said, "Be of good cheer! It is I; do not be afraid" (Mat. 14:27; Mk. 6:50).
4. Again, to his disciples, in the Upper Room, on the eve of his crucifixion, he said, "Be of good cheer, I have overcome the world" (John 16:33).
5. Finally, in Acts 22:11, he said to Paul, "Be of good cheer, Paul . . . you will be my witness in Rome."

Paul believed Jesus. So should we. Paul did go to Rome. The Apostle completed that which God had called him to accomplish. The Lord will do the same for us as we yield our lives to him. "Be of good cheer!"

b. BEING BLESSED

Blessings are an important part of the life of a Christian. God has indeed blessed each one of us beyond measure. Even in our times of testing, we have to admit that we are blessed and have most of what we need, if not all that we need for the moment.

Within the pages of Scripture we find many blessings, and in religious tradition you will find blessings for food and wine and blessings for smelling fragrant oils, fruits, and plants. There are even blessings for sight and hearing. Perhaps the most intriguing of all is found in Numbers 6:24–26, called the Priestly Blessing or Aaron's Blessing.

"The Lord bless thee, and keep thee:
The Lord make his face shine upon thee, and
be gracious unto thee:
The Lord lift up his countenance upon thee,
and give thee peace." (KJV)

Daily, priests would ascend to a special platform, cover their heads with the prayer shawl, and with outstretched arms recite the ancient blessing. The blessing was recited daily by the priests.

Aaron's Blessing contains 15 words in the Hebrew text. The first phrase contains 3 words; the second phrase 5 words; the last phrase 7 words. It ascends gradually, asking first of all for material blessing, then spiritual blessing, finally climaxing in a petition for God's greatest gift, namely, peace.

"The Lord bless thee . . . the Lord make his face shine upon thee . . . the Lord lift up his countenance upon thee" is saying the same thing. To be blessed by the Lord is to behold his "face," his "countenance" resulting in security, grace and peace which is totality of completeness and purpose.

Therefore, the blessing points the pilgrim to a personal encounter with God. This is the only way to find true peace. How can someone have a personal encounter with God? Jesus said, "I am the way, the truth, and the life. No one comes to the Father except through me" (John 14:6). By faith, believe and receive Jesus Christ into your life and receive the greatest blessing: eternal life. "Believe on the Lord Jesus Christ and you will be saved" (Acts 16:31). "Peace I leave with you, my peace I give to you; not as the world gives do I give to you. Let not your heart be troubled, neither let it be afraid" (John 14:27).

The Lord Jesus became the "Passover lamb," the atonement for sin. The prophet stated that the Messiah "was wounded for our transgressions, [that] he was bruised for our iniquities: the chastisement of our peace was upon him; and with his stripes we are healed" (Isaiah 53:5, KJV).

As a result of the cross, one can have a personal encounter with God through the shed blood of the Messiah, the Lord Jesus, by trusting in him alone for salvation.

Jesus said he was the Messiah and his life, death, and resurrection were proof. It is only through the Messiah, the Lord Jesus, that you and I can fully understand and experience Aaron's Blessing in finding true provision, purpose, and peace.

c. BODY, SOUL, SPIRIT

"And may your whole spirit, soul, and body be preserved blameless at the coming of our Lord Jesus Christ."

—1 Thess. 5:23

You are specially designed by God. Your strengths and weaknesses are not randomly selected components. You are alive at this time, in your family, your home, your city, your country, on this planet, in this universe for a very important reason. The Scripture teaches that you are "fearfully and wonderfully made" and that before you were born your days were "ordained" and written in God's "book" (Psa. 139:13–16). The Apostle Paul mentions that we have a body, soul, and spirit. What does this mean?

Body

"The Lord God formed the man from the dust of the ground and breathed into his nostrils the breath of life, and the man became a living soul."

—Gen. 2:7, KJV

Jewish mystics have believed that man arose from the area where the Temple stood. That being the case, a little more light is shed on the following words that Paul penned: "Do you not know that your body is a temple of the Holy Spirit, who is in you, whom you have received from God?" (1 Cor. 6:19)

We have been given a certain amount of days. "The length of our days is seventy years—or eighty, if we have the strength" (Psa. 90:10). We would be wise to "number our days," realizing that "time is short" (Psa. 90:12).

Soul

The soul is that which gives life to the body, that which causes movement and has consciousness. Generally, a reference to life in Scripture or the life of an individual refers to the soul—"He's alive!" (Acts 20:10; 1 Pet. 3:20) The soul enables us to perceive and conclude ideas concrete and abstract in nature with the ability to make decisions and analyze (Matt. 11:29; Acts 14:2; Rom. 2:9–11). Animals have souls (life for life, or soul for soul, according to Lev. 24:18). Basically, the soul is any animated creature, human or other (1 Cor. 15:45; Rev. 16:3). It is truly a good thing to value life, for it is true that "life is precious."

Spirit

The breath from God (Gen. 2:7) breathed into man's nostrils separates him from the animals. Animals do not have God's breath; only human beings. It is this spirit, not to be confused with the Holy Spirit, which enables one to comprehend God.

With the soul we can think, study, reason, and conclude. Through the spirit we can have "spiritual intellect," or the ability to understand the things of God. It is an intuitive realization of the truth of God and the enabling to understand the mystery of the divine. Separate from our reasoning, intellect, and rational mind, the spirit empowers us to seek after God and to choose good over evil—animals cannot.

The breath of God makes it possible for human beings to understand, trust, believe, and then truly seek after God. Simply, it is through our spirit (the breath from God) that enables us to, if you will, link up with the Holy Spirit who causes regeneration, or causes one to be born again. Animals cannot experience this event (Jn. 3:8; 2 Thess. 2:8; Rom. 8:1–17; John 3:3–21; Rom. 3:11; 1 Cor. 2). For example, the minister is preaching. As a result, the Holy Spirit convicts the human heart (the spirit, or breath from God) regarding the need to be born again. The person is able to believe and comprehend God because indwelling in that person is the spirit, or breath from God. This person was dead in their trespasses and sins without Christ and now has been made alive in Christ (Eph. 2; Col. 2). Their spirit was dead because of the sin of Adam and now it has been quickened, or made alive, because of the blood sacrifice of the Lamb of God (Rom. 5:12; Rom. 6:23; Heb. 9). Animals are unable to experience this regeneration (Jn. 6:44; Jn. 16:5–15). An amazing mystery!

We are wonderfully made in God's image. May we value each day as a gift from God, realizing he holds us by our hand and at the same time we are held in his hand (Isa. 41:13; Jn.10:28).

d. CHURCH UNDERSTOOD

The church is both the body and the bride of Christ, according to the Scripture. Christ is the head of the body (Col. 1:18); he is also the bridegroom of the bride (Mat. 9:15; Rev. 21:2). He founded the church and purchased it with his blood. The church is the only institution founded by Christ. As a result, believers can enjoy the fellowship of faith with one another and believers can enjoy serving together in the gospel.

Believers observe two ordinances: baptism and the Lord's Supper. (Others also include feet washing). Believers within the church exercise their gifts received from the Holy Spirit in order to extend the gospel throughout the world.

The word "church" is from the Greek *ekklesia*, which is composed of two other Greek words: *ek* ("out of") and *kalein* ("to call"), simply meaning called out ones or assembly.

Prior to the New Testament, the word had two general uses. In the secular Greek, it was used to designate the assembly of the citizens of a self-governing Greek city (Acts 19:39–41). For example, Ephesus was granted the privilege of self-rule, but within the framework of the Laws of the Roman Empire.

In the Greek translation of the Old Testament, the Septuagint, the word translated the Hebrew word *qahal*, referring to the nation of Israel assembled before God and under his direct theocratic rule (Deut. 31:30; Jud. 21:8).

Therefore, the word "church" in the New Testament never refers to organized Christianity or to a group of churches. It denotes either a local body of baptized believers or includes all the redeemed throughout all the ages. The greater emphasis in the New Testament is on the local church.

In Matthew 16, following Peter's confession—"Thou art the Christ, the Son of the living God"—Jesus said these words: "On this rock (the rock of Peter's confession of the identity of Christ) (Upon me, upon the truth of who I am) I will build my church, and the gates of Hades shall not prevail against it" (Matt. 16:18). The disciples were aware of the dual use of the word *ekklesia* in both the Greek and Hebrew sense. So, in effect, Jesus said, "The Greeks have their church, and the Hebrews have their church. Now, I will build my church, and the gates of Hades shall not prevail against it."

This remark about Hades is often interpreted to mean that Hell or evil will not overcome or stand up against the church. This idea is true.

However, this is not what Jesus said here. The Greek reads, "And the gates of Hades shall not have strength against it." Hades is the abode of the dead. Gates are used either to keep out or to keep in. Those outside Hades are not trying to get in; those inside are trying to get out. These gates shall not be able to hold Christ's people in the abode of the dead. Therefore, this is a promise of the resurrection.

The point is that Christ's church shall live on after physical death. In Ephesians 3: 10-11, Paul said that the eternal purpose of God in Christ is to be declared by or through the church. So the church stands at the center of God's redemptive purpose in Christ.

The church in the general sense is made up of those redeemed through Christ. The local church is composed of baptized believers. The mission of the church is to spread the gospel of redemption to a lost world.

Paul states in Philippians 3:20, "For our citizenship is in heaven." Moffatt translates it, "But we are a colony of heaven." Under the Roman system, certain cities were rewarded for faithful service by being made colonies of Rome. Their citizens so lived as to cause others to desire to become Romans. They were, if you will, little bits of Rome set down in the Empire.

Paul said that the church at Philippi was such a colony—they were a colony of Heaven. It was a little bit of Heaven set down in a pagan world. Its citizens were to permeate its environment with the principles of heaven and each member should so live as to cause all others to wish to become citizens of God's kingdom. May this be said of our local church!

Non-church people will hear what church people do and how they live before they hear what church people say. Church people, please live godly lives in Christ Jesus, be witnesses in your neighborhood, and send others—anointed of God and trained properly—to the uttermost part of the world.

Church missions can be summarized by an acrostic: the word LIFE. Christians are to

L Love and worship God

I Instruct from and study his Word

F Fellowship with believers and care for one another

E Evangelize the world by sharing the gospel will all people

*"I have come that they may have life,
and that they may have it more abundantly."*

—Jesus (John 10:10)

e. DRAWING IN MIRACLES

Sometimes we feel like there is no hope. The doctor gave us a bad report, or the financial need is greater than realized. At times, despair seems to overwhelm us. Nothing short of a miracle will help. Sometimes our feeling of being overwhelmed can blind us to what is right in front of us.

The Scripture tells us that the universe is governed by established laws. However, God or God's messengers can perform acts that defy such laws. We call these acts miracles.

There is a story in the Bible that describes the wife of Obadiah, who found herself deeply in debt after her husband's death (2 Kings 4:2). Her husband was a student of the prophets, perhaps preparing for the ministry, who loved the Lord passionately. He died, apparently prematurely, and the creditors were knocking on her door, threatening to take her two boys as slaves to pay off the debt. This was common practice in that day.

She pleaded with Elisha to help her. Elisha asked, "What do you have in your house?" She replied, "Nothing, except a little oil." I assume this was olive oil, as it is plentiful in this part of the world.

The prophet told her to go to her neighbors and ask for a lot of empty jars. Then he said, "Go inside your house and begin to fill the jars with your oil." She filled each jar to the brim. She asked for another jar, but there was no jar left. So she filled each of the many jars she gathered, sold the oil, paid off her debt, and had enough left over for her and her two sons. No one knows how much oil she originally had. Some say little; some would say as minute as to smear on the little finger. Whatever the amount, a miracle took place.

If the prophet alone had the power to perform the miracle, why did he ask the woman, "What do you have in your house?" Good question! Was it necessary for her to have a small amount of oil for the miracle to occur? Yes.

There had to be a starting point for the miracle to take place. Jesus would do a similar thing in John chapter 2, turning six jars of water into wine. There had to be something tangible to be the point of reference for the miracle.

God has given each of us a little oil, or empty jars—something that he can use and miraculously transform from paucity to plenty. We simply need to emulate Obadiah's wife by moving forward and start pouring, believing that something will happen.

f. EARLY WILL I SEEK YOU

"O God, you are my God; Early will I seek you; My soul thirsts for you; My flesh longs for you in a dry and thirsty land where there is no water. So I have looked for you in the sanctuary, to see your power and your glory. Because your loving kindness is better than life, my lips shall praise you."

—PSALM 63:1–3

A short distance from the outskirts of Jerusalem and Bethlehem begins the Judean Desert. To say it looks like another planet is an understatement. Limestone mountains, hills, sand, rocks, scattered shrubs, and an occasional olive or fig tree, perhaps a palm tree, highlight the region. Temperatures can soar as high as 120 degrees.

Animal life is present, as you will find in the hills and mountains ibex (a mountain goat-like creature with beautiful horns), hyrax or coney (a beaver-looking rodent), lizards, snakes, donkeys, and the like. With the tent-dwelling Bedouins, you will usually find camels, horses, goats, sheep, and every now and then a satellite dish so they can watch CNN.

The Jordan River cuts through the parched soil with its cool flowing mountain water and lush rich vegetation along the banks. To find an oasis is wonderful, as it represents the life-giving source. En-Gedi, near Qumran and Masada, located by the Dead Sea, is perhaps the most famous oasis in the desert, with its beautiful waterfall, trickling stream, cliffs, trees, wildlife, shade, and cool breezes. You may recall that David and his men lodged there finding refreshment and safety from Saul (1 Samuel 23–24).

A person could easily perish without having water and food in this barren place. To know where these few precious water sources are located or to know where to find nourishment is a precious gift. The wilderness is a brutal place. To survive is to know what to do.

David

David wrote a psalm while in the Judean Desert. Endeavoring not to perish, he discovered the secret of the holy men and prophets of old. He came to a point where he no longer desired food and water; rather, in the crucible of the desert, he found his passion was for a greater source of sustenance. Let's take a look into David's heart and see what he discovered.

O God, you are my God. With a passion of a lover, he is claiming, "I am yours and you are mine."

Early will I seek you. With great earnest I desire you. When I wake, you are the first one on my mind. When a person loves God with a passion, he is on their mind constantly.

My soul thirsts for you. Soul refers to the emotions, the personality, that which is your reason and intellect. In other words, as one who would desperately look for water in the wilderness, David is feeling after God, seeking Him with every ounce of strength, emotion, and reason within his being. It is truly a matter of survival.

My flesh longs for you. In this parched land, your body begins to dehydrate and your skin begins to wither and shrivel, becoming like leather. You are dying and at times don't realize it. You can become delirious, lightheaded, wandering in circles. Utter dryness and thirst and exhaustion describe this setting. When the wilderness circumstances hit us hard, only God can give life, sustain life, and refresh life.

In a dry and thirsty land where there is no water. The wilderness reminds us of the world and its offering of happiness. One quickly discovers there is a void, a hole that develops in the world. It is dry and you will become thirsty because there is no life-giving source in the world's treasury of hope. Only God can fill that void and bring true purpose.

So I have looked for you in the sanctuary to see your power and your glory. At this time, King David was physically separated from the ark. The ark was where the formal version of worship took place. David had seen the evidence of God's presence in the sanctuary in Jerusalem. It was an expression of his eagerness to seek God, to feel close to him. Often times we do the same thing. To sit in the quietness of the sanctuary (worship center) is an experience that can be gratifying. However, David is discovering something even more important, found in the next verse.

Because your loving kindness is better than life, my lips shall praise you. Loving kindness reflects the idea of *hesed*, which is mercy, kindness, hope, and blessing, coming from God. Because of this, David says, "I will lift up my hands in your name" (verse 4).

God's blessing and mercy are "better than life." If all we have is *hesed*, that is enough. It is sufficient, no matter our circumstances.

Esau

In contrast, we find another story in the Scripture concerning a wilderness experience. Esau came back home after being in the wilderness hunting food. He was exhausted, famished, and focused upon one thing: his stomach.

And Esau said to Jacob, "Please feed me" (Genesis 25:30). In ancient times, the head of the tribe or clan, usually the firstborn, acted as the priest. That position was purely spiritual. Esau was anything but spiritual. He was fickle, impulsive, self-gratifying, guilty of hyperbole ("I am about to die," verse 32), and not interested in spiritual things. Had his birthright involved material compensation, he would not have so easily given it up.

His uncontrolled appetite revealed his true colors. His heart was preoccupied with only his own selfish needs. His nobility paled in comparison to one who is worthy of being the spiritual head of the clan. He lost his birthright in order to fill his stomach. It was not enough for him; he wanted more. It was all about him.

Better than Life

In looking at these two accounts, it is obvious to see the contrast between the fulfillment David found and the temporary fulfillment Esau found. David gained life while Esau lost everything. Esau lived his life continually striving to fill his stomach, endeavoring to find contentment and coming up short in the wilderness of life. David, in his wilderness experience, discovered the most important truth of all.

Hesed—God's mercy, grace, hope, and blessing—is "better than life." If this is the only blessing we have in life, then one blessing is enough. It is sufficient!

g. ENLARGE THY TENT

In Isaiah 54:1–3, the prophet reminds us of several principles that apply to our life. Recognizing that the context of the passage refers to Israel, the principles can be applied to your circumstances.

Verse 1 focuses on laboring years. Verse 2 talks about the days or months that are immediately before you. Verse 3 addresses the ramifications of one's labor.

Your life has significance and the future is in God's hands!

In verse 2, Isaiah mentions four factors that can harness the full potential of our lives. Certain foundations must be laid. They are as follows:

1. "Enlarge thy tent."

    That is, prepare for the harvest of blessing that is coming.

2. "Stretch forth the curtains."

    God always multiplies what he has. A day of stretching is upon us, for this is good!

3. "Spare not."

    This has to do with vision. Your vision must be positive and big, not limiting what God can do and wants to do with your life.

4. "Lengthen thy cords, and strengthen thy stakes."

    Dig deep spiritual foundations, such as prayer, dedication to God's Word, and building a genuine relationship with God.

If you embrace these four steps, the consequence for your life will be that of having a profound impact upon the world. This is the promise of verse 3.

h. I AM JESUS

"And Joseph said to his brothers, 'Please come near to me.' So they came near. Then he said: 'I am Joseph your brother.'"

—Genesis 45:4

After 20 years, Joseph revealed himself to his brothers. His revelation was simple: he said, "I am Joseph." That was it. How very simple!

The Gospel is very simple that a child can understand. God so loved the world that he sent his only Son to die on a cross for our sins. He was buried and rose again the third day.

1,700 years later, another Jew was determined to crush a new sect that believed that Jesus of Nazareth, an executed man, was the long-awaited Messiah of Israel and the world. On his way to Damascus, with the sole purpose of sifting out these believers bringing them to justice and death, a blinding light shone round about him.

Falling off his horse, laying prostrate on the ground and trembling, he cried, "Who are you, Lord?" The answer was simple: "I am Jesus." That was it—"I am Jesus." In one moment, Saul was a changed man. He went from sinner to saint, from blasphemer to believer, from persecutor to preacher.

"I am Joseph."

"I am Jesus."

Salvation is not a difficult process. When the time is ripe, God the Holy Spirit reveals God the Son to a person's soul in such a simple way.

Joseph said, "Please come near to me."

Jesus said, "Come to me, all you who labor and are heavy laden, and I will give you rest…learn from me, for I am gentle and lowly in heart, and you will find rest for your souls" (Matthew 11:28–29).

Dear friend, come to Jesus and trust and believe in him alone and you will find what you are looking for.

i. ISRAEL: "ONE WHO STRIVES WITH GOD"

Genesis 32:28

Before the world was created, and before the stars danced in majestic design…

Before the galaxies displayed their glorious splendor, and before Adam and Eve graced the landscape of our blue jeweled planet…

Before there was light or darkness, and before anything was realized, before time itself…

…there was God.

Within the eternal mind of God, before anything was created in Heaven or on earth, visible or invisible, there was a plan, there was a design, and a purpose that he set in motion.

You see, he is before all things, and in him all things consist. And Christ is the head of the body—the church—who is the beginning, the firstborn from the dead, that in all things he may have the preeminence (Col. 2).

God Communicates

The God who created all life chose to communicate. He chose to communicate through his creation. David said, "The Heavens declare the glory of God and the firmament shows his handiwork" (Ps. 91:1). Just by simply looking up into the heavens, you know that God exists and is there.

God chose to communicate through his Word. The psalmist wrote, "Forever, O Lord, your word is settled in heaven. Your faithfulness endures to all generations; you established the earth and it stands" (Ps. 119:89).

David stated, "You have magnified your word above all" (Ps. 138:2).

God chose to communicate through a particular people. Nearly 4,000 years ago, God chose a 75-year-old man from Mesopotamia and made a covenant with him. Abraham lived some 300 years after the Flood, and Jewish tradition maintains that his mother took him as a child to learn from Noah and Shem, as they were still alive during Abraham's lifetime.

God made a covenant with Abraham (Genesis 12:1–3). When the Lord made this covenant, he began to communicate specifically through a chosen people. These chosen people were the descendants of Abraham and Sarah. Through Abraham came the promised son Isaac. Then Jacob was born, then the 12 sons of Jacob (the patriarchs), followed by Moses, the prophets, judges, and kings.

Profound Promise

God conveyed a story through these descendants of Abraham—a story so wonderful, so profound, so simple and yet so complex. It was a story of an Anointed One that would come, a Messiah who would redeem Israel and deliver them from their oppressors. This Messiah would be the glory of Israel and a light to the Gentiles.

Provocative Land

God also disclosed a promise concerning land that exclusively belonged to the descendants of Isaac, Abraham's son. This hope touched the very soul within the children of Israel. This promised piece of real estate is at the heart of the tension throughout the Middle East. Who owns the land is the main issue that is so provocative that people are willing to give their lives for this chunk of property.

Abraham had another son through Hagar named Ishmael. Ishmael's descendants are the Arabs. Isaac's descendants are the Jews. The piece of real estate promised is called Israel. The question of who owns the land is, among other things, a religious issue, not political. The descendants of Isaac say they own the land; the descendants of Ishmael say the land belongs to them.

Both Isaac and Ishmael are children of Abraham. The Jews claim the land promised to them is found within the writings of Scripture written by Moses some 1,500 years before Christ. The Moslem Abram's claim to the land is found within the writings of the Koran, written centuries after Christ (Sura 2:124–129), where they believe that Abraham bound Ishmael—not Isaac—on the altar on Mt. Moriah (Gen. 22). Thus, the Moslem believes that all the promises of inheritance and blessing would fall upon the descendants of Ishmael, the firstborn of Abraham.

What area does God describe as His chosen land?

- Genesis 15:18 (from the river of Egypt to the Euphrates)

This is the same location as Israel today. In fact, Israel does not have all the land promised her. The fulfillment of all the land is yet to come.

Whom did God choose to dwell in this land?

- Genesis 12:1–3 (descendants of Abraham)

This covenant was later confirmed to Abraham to be unconditional and everlasting (Genesis 17:7–8). Subsequently, this covenant was confirmed to his son Isaac in Genesis 17:19, and then to his grandson Jacob in Genesis 35:9–15.

God chose the descendants of Isaac, Abraham's son, to be

1. A witness to the true God of the universe before the nations
2. A conduit to receive, preserve, and transmit Holy Scripture
3. The posterity for the Messiah, the savior of the world

God chose Eretz Yisrael (the land of Israel) to be the center of the world.

Israel has been on the crossroads of the great empires, Assyria, Babylonia, Egypt, Greece, and Rome. Israel has been "God's testing ground of faith." Israel has been—and still is—the place where God shows his miraculous power to sustain and bless his ancient people. God's covenant regarding the land is everlasting and unconditional.

God said to Abram, "For all the land which you see I give to you and your descendants forever . . . Arise, walk in the land through its length and its width, for I give it to you" (Gen. 13:15–17).

Promise of Return

Because of disobedience, the Jewish nation was dispersed throughout the world (Josh. 23:14–16). However, there was a promise of return: "Therefore, behold, the days are coming,' says the Lord, 'that they shall no longer say, "As the Lord lives who brought up the children of Israel from the land of Egypt," but "As the Lord lives who brought up and led the descendants of the house of Israel from the north country and from all the countries where I had driven them." And they shall dwell in their own land'" (Jer. 23:7–8).

"Behold, I will bring them from the north country, and gather them from the ends of the earth . . . I will lead them . . . I am a Father to Israel . . . Hear the word of the Lord, O nations . . . He who scattered Israel will gather him" (Jer. 31:8-10).

Gentiles Will Help

"For the Lord will have mercy on Jacob, and will still choose Israel, and settle them in their own land. The strangers (Gentiles) will be joined with them . . . People (Gentiles) will take them and bring them to their place" (Isa. 14:1–2).

"Behold, I will lift my hand in an oath to the nations (Gentiles), and set my banner for the peoples: They shall bring your sons in their arms, and your daughters shall be carried on their shoulders" (Isa. 49:22).

Salvation Will Come

"For I will take you from among the nations, gather you out of all countries, and bring you into your own land. Then I will sprinkle clean water on you, and you shall be clean . . . I will give you a new heart . . . I will put my Spirit within you . . . Then you shall dwell in the land that I gave to your fathers; you shall be my people, and I will be your God" (Ezek. 36:24–28).

Never to be Rejected

"This is what the Lord says, he who appoints the sun to shine by day, who decrees the moon and stars to shine by night, who stirs up the sea so that its waves roar—the Lord Almighty is his name: Only if these decrees vanish from my sight, declares the Lord, will the descendants of Israel ever cease to be a nation before me. This is what the Lord says: Only if the heavens above can be measured and the foundations of the earth below be searched out will I reject all the descendants of Israel because of all they have done, declares the Lord" (Jer. 31:35–37, NIV).

Precious Promises

"I will make you a great nation; I will bless you and make your name great and you shall be a blessing. I will bless those who bless you, and I will curse him who curses you; and in you all the families of the earth shall be blessed" (Gen. 12:1–3).

j. KNOWN IN THE GATES

Proverbs 31:23

Life comes at us pretty hard! The moments that define who we are can be blessings or, at times, overwhelming circumstances. Raising families, embarking on our careers, and simply living life takes years of nurturing, planning, and praying. As much as we would like to think we are rugged, independent individuals, we simply cannot do life alone. We need each other, and most importantly, we need God.

The Key

There is a key ingredient that connects us with God: certainty. Believing that God exists and was manifested in Christ, having certainty of the truth that God can be known not only intellectually but personally, is key to having peace within your soul.

The woman of faith found in Proverbs 31 had a husband that was "known in the gates." In Hebrew, "gates" (*she'arim*) not only refers to a door but also connotes to "reveal" or "to think" or "to be known." "Her husband is known in the gates" has a deeper meaning: God is known and revealed to those who believe with certainty.

The Word "Flawless"

In the previous chapter of Proverbs, we read, "Every word of God is flawless" (Proverbs 30:5), meaning that it is pure, tested, and refined. John writes, "And the Word became flesh and dwelt among us, and we saw his glory," referring to Jesus (John 1:14). Messiah Jesus is the Word manifested in flesh—he is flawless, pure, tested, and refined.

We Can Know

Heaven and heaven of heavens cannot contain God, and his glory is above earth and heaven. He is great and we know him not. We cannot find him out, and his footsteps are not known. Great is the Lord, and greatly to be praised; his greatness is unsearchable—there is no searching of his understanding, and God fills heaven and earth—yet we can know the unsearchable through faith, belief and certainty (1 Kg. 8:27; Ps. 148:13; Job 36:26, 37:23; Ps.77:19, 145:3; Isa. 40:28; Jer. 23:24; Eph. 3:8).

With Certainty

With certainty we know that Messiah Jesus is the "gate" God revealed, becoming flesh, who is the True Light who lightens everyone who believes. (John 10:7, 8:12, 1:9). With certainty we know that God will never forsake you, leaving you stranded alone (Deut. 31:6, 8; Josh. 1:5; Heb. 13:5).

No matter what comes at you in life, you have a redeemer, friend, and protector. With certainty you can believe the flawless Word: "Then Jesus again spoke to them, saying, 'I am the Light of the world; he who follows me will not walk in the darkness, but will have the Light of life. Truly, truly, I say to you, I am the door of the sheep, if anyone enters through me, he will be saved, and will go in and out and find pasture. I am the way, the truth, and the life; no one comes to the Father but through me" (John 8:12, 10:7, 9, 14:6).

With certainty, "[h]er husband (was) known in the gates," and with certainty we can know God in Christ, and even though God is certainly beyond our complete comprehension at this time, one day, face-to-face, we shall know fully God's splendor for those who believe and put their faith in Messiah Jesus for salvation (1 Cor. 13:12).

k. LIFE

"I am come that they might have life."

—JOHN 10:10

We have been given a great gift, namely the gift of life! "And the Lord God formed man of the dust of the ground, and breathed into his nostrils the breath of life; and man became a living soul" (Genesis 2:7, KJV). By virtue of this act, man has been given a special relationship with his creator. "Man alone has the breath of life blown into his nostrils by God himself. Only by virtue of this direct animation did man become a living being, drawing directly from God his life source."[1] Paul stated on Mars Hill in Athens before the philosophers that God "giveth to all life, and breath . . . for in him we live, and move and have our being" (Acts 17:25, 28, KJV).

Different from the Beasts

We are different from the beasts of the field in that beasts react instinctively while humans express "intellect, free will, self-awareness, consciousness of the existence of others, conscience, responsibility and self control."[2] Therefore, human life is precious and has purpose. David writes, "For I am fearfully and wonderfully made . . . how precious also are thy thoughts unto me" (Psalm 139:14, 17, KJV). Beloved, remember: You are here this hour, this minute, this second, in this universe, on this planet for a reason. You are no mistake—God makes no mistakes.

One scholar makes this observation of the Hebrew word "life" (*HaYYiM* or HYYM—there are no vowels in Hebrew, simply vowel sounds): "The word for life in Hebrew ends with (*YiM*), the grammatical indicator of plurality. We are granted not one life, but two."[3]

Name of God

Indeed, this scholar is correct in his statement, as truly we "are granted" two lives. One life is spent here on earth, and the other will be spent in eternity. In terms of eternity, the Scripture speaks of two eternal places of existence—namely, Heaven or Hell. This Jewish scholar continues his statement by saying, "Central to the word *HaYYiM* (the Hebrew word for 'life'), are two YYs (two 'yuds,' the smallest of Hebrew letters) which, combined, form the name of God."[4]

Now here is an interesting thought! Central to the Hebrew word for "life" is the name of God. The Apostle John tells us that Jesus is the very essence of "life" (John 1:3, 4). Jesus is God, and those who trust in him alone as Savior and Messiah will spend eternity in the presence of God, who is central to all life. Jesus said, "I am the way, the truth, and the life: no man cometh unto the Father, but by me" (John 14:6, KJV). John also stated, "He that believeth on the Son hath everlasting life: and he that believeth not the Son shall not see life: but the wrath of God abideth on him" (John 3:36, KJV).

Endnotes

1. Sarna, Nahum M. *Understanding Genesis: The Heritage of Biblical Israel.* New York: Schocken Books, 1970.
2. Ibid.
3. Blech, Benjamin. *The Secrets of Hebrew Words.* New Jersey: Jason Aronson, Inc., 1991.
4. Ibid.

1. THE SILENT GOD

"Lord, where are you? I cried out to you over and over again. You have been silent! Where are you?"

Christians may face the challenge of God's silence. You know, when the illness comes, when there is financial difficulty, when you are having relational problems, when you meet emotional challenges, when you fall into a spiritual depression, when you are faced with temptation—where is God? Why is he silent? All believers in Jesus will face tests and trials somewhere along their journey.

Where is God? Do you find, at times, when you cry out to him, he is silent? I have.

When God reveals himself, it is purely an act of grace through his Spirit. It isn't that God is silent; it is, however, that he chooses to reveal himself to his children at specific times. When he does reveal his purpose in your life, it is usually very clear and sometimes sudden.

Consider God appearing to Moses in the burning bush. It wasn't until Moses experienced an incredible season of trial and testing that God revealed his purpose (Exodus 3).

Look at Elijah after his victory on the mountain. He was exhausted and depressed ready to die when suddenly an angel touched him (1 Kings 19).

During a time of mourning, Isaiah was in the Temple and the Lord was revealed to him. His purpose was made clear and his path was set in motion. He now had clear direction and understanding of his circumstances (Isaiah 6).

It was during a time of civil and political upheaval that young Jeremiah heard from God. God assured him that he was on this earth during this time, during this occasion, for a purpose. Jeremiah was set in motion once he understood from God why the times were they way they were. It now made sense to this weeping prophet (Jeremiah 1).

Ruth suffered the death of her husband and experienced great loss. She found God in the process and yet still suffered hardship until the Lord replenished her life with blessing (Ruth 1:16, 4:10–14).

Esther found that she was brought into the kingdom for such a time as this. What was this special time? It was a time of political turmoil in which the Jews would face extermination unless someone intervened. She found out that God orchestrated events in order to bring about something greater than herself. It wasn't an easy task before her. In fact, her life could have been taken from her if she failed. She prayed and asked others to pray. It worked, for God answered (Esther 4).

The priest Zacharias was going about his daily duties of the Temple, troubled, when he finally heard from God. He and his wife were both righteous before Lord. They loved God and yet they had a test in their lives. Their burden was that Elizabeth was barren, a curse in that culture. So they prayed and prayed to God. He was silent for so long and then suddenly God spoke through the angel Gabriel.

It startled Zacharias. In fact, he did not believe that God was answering his prayers. After all, it has been so long. Why now? He wasn't sure what to make of it all (Luke 1).

At the Pool of Bethesda, there was a man with an infirmity desiring to be healed. He had been living with this infirmity for 38 years. For almost four decades, he suffered. He prayed and waited, prayed and waited. Then Jesus saw him. For almost 40 years, there was silence. Then God appeared in the flesh (John 5).

Stephen, a man of faith, Spirit-filled, was living out his faith. He was put to death for his belief in Jesus. It wasn't until moments before he passed into the eternal that he saw Jesus and understood that he was in the perfect will of God, standing true to the faith (Acts 7).

Beloved, do you see a pattern here? Being a Christian, being a follower of God, does not mean that you will be trouble-free. In every case, the believer experienced obstacles and valleys, and sometimes it cost them their lives. Months, years, decades pass, then God speaks and it is clear regarding the question "Why?"

It seems to me that the propensity of God is to be silent. It is an act of grace and love. His silence strengthens our faith. "Faith is the substance of things hoped for, the evidence of things not seen" (Hebrews 11:1, KJV).

Is God there? Yes! He is Emmanuel, God with us. You can see him in the sidereal universe (Psalm 19:1). You can see him in the gift of children (Luke 18:15–17). He is there in every breath you take (Acts 17:25). Every changed life is a testimony to the fact that God is there (2 Corinthians 5:17). Every miracle points us to God (Luke 1:37).

Sometimes we cannot see because our hearts are not clean. When we humble our hearts before him and seek him and confess our sin, he will cleanse our hearts and we will see him (Hebrews 12:14; 1 John 1:8–10). To seek the path of peace, holiness, and love is a difficult road. It is not natural for human beings to do so. It is only through his spirit seeking to follow his Christ shall we see God, for Christ is God (1 John 4:4; Hebrews 11:6).

Therefore beloved, when God is silent, remember that he is there. He promised that he will never leave nor forsake us (Hebrews 13:5).

When God is silent, it is an act of grace and love to strengthen our faith (Hebrews 11:1).

When God is silent, he has a greater purpose in mind, though we may not fully understand (Romans 8:28-39).

When God is silent, the Spirit will make intercession for us, for we do not know what to pray (Romans 8:26–27).

When God is silent, we are to wait and hope for that which we do not see nor understand (Romans 8:24–25; Isaiah 40:31)

When God is silent, do not despair, for at the exact moment, when the time is right, he will speak, and you will know what it means to seek him.

"Shall not the Judge of all the earth do right?"

—Genesis 18:25, KJV

"Blessed be the Lord God of Israel for ever and ever. And all the people said, 'Amen,' and praised the Lord."

—1 Chronicles 16:36, KJV

m. SPIRITUALITY AND BIBLE STUDY

Without continued contact with the Book, the Jews instinctively knew they could not attain self-fulfillment or even survive as a people. The Scripture exempted no one, not even a king of Israel, from studying the Scripture (Deut. 17:18–19). Joshua likewise was instructed to apply himself to the Word of God (Jos. 1:8). Abraham's descendants did not regard reading the Scripture as simply a luxury. To them, it was as necessary to life as eating or sleeping. It is said around the dinner table of the rabbis that if ever there were to be a moment that the Word of God was not studied on the earth, God would turn the universe back again into primordial chaos, or void, that preceded the creation of the world. Their point is well taken. This manuscript addresses the passion of the Hebraic background of Christian faith.

The pursuit of truth is very important to the religious Jew. Truth is the totality of all there is, and Christianity points to the fact that Jesus said he was the Truth manifested in the flesh. For his followers, he prayed, "Sanctify them through thy truth: Thy Word is truth."

Psalm 119 records at least 5 truths regarding the power of Bible study:

1. It opens our eyes and changes our life (verse 18).
2. It brings stability and wisdom (verses 98, 110, 114–117).
3. It brings understanding and insight (verse 99).
4. Spiritual maturity results (verse 100).
5. Righteousness results (verse 11).

n. SPIRITUALITY AND PRAYER

In Acts chapter 2, we find the disciples together devoting themselves to the reading and teaching of the Word, worship, and prayer. Very simply, prayer is a natural byproduct resulting from Bible study and worship. Prayer is communicating with God. He communicates to us through his Word. Communion with God unfolds in our spirit was we think on him—thus we begin to worship. Subsequently, we begin to flesh out our spiritual journey with God, praising him, petitioning him, and thanking him. This is called prayer. As one reads through this book and sincerely pursues the spiritual disciplines found therein, one will being a journey that leads to godliness as well as discovering many important components to Christian faith and practice being found in Christ Jesus.

o. SPIRITUALITY AND WORSHIP

Worship is a verb that calls for action, vibrancy, and participation. Psalm 95 opens with an invitation to worship. Worship occurs only when we find ourselves meeting with God and within our spirit we begin praising him for his love, wisdom, beauty, truth, holiness, compassion, mercy, grace, power, and so forth.

The main reason behind the creation of human life and all things is to worship God! The Bible answers over and over again that all these things have been designed by God to worship and praise him (Nehemiah 9:6; Philippians 2:9–11).

When we worship God, we acknowledge his holiness.

According to the Scripture, it is in the realm of holiness that worship of the Lord takes place (1 Chronicles 16:28-29). How foolish it is to think that we could come into the presence of God with sin or corruption in our hearts! Sin always mars our fellowship with God. The holiness of God should motivate us to fall down before God and worship him.

The place where we worship him becomes sacred.

The place where the body of Christ worships becomes sacred because of what takes place there. This is supported throughout Scripture. There was a sacredness atmosphere attached to the place of worship because of the nature of the One being worshiped. Yes, it is true that the believer's body is the temple of the Holy Spirit, but that does not eliminate the seriousness of the place of worship, no matter where it is.

Worship is the precious relationship between the believer and God.

This fact makes all other pursuits secondary and gives meaning to everything that is thought, said, or done. Jesus said it this way, "The hour is coming, and now is, when the true worshipers will worship the Father in spirit and truth; for the Father is seeking such to worship him. God is Spirit, and those who worship him must worship him in spirit and truth" (John 4:23). What Jesus is referring to here is the contrast between what goes on inside of you and what you do on the outside.

Believers worship God in the Spirit (Phil. 3:3).

God is seeking those who will worship him. Biblically speaking, worshipping God is a lifestyle that encompasses our whole being, day in and day out—what we say, what we do, and most importantly how we do it. God is not so interested in the quantity of worship. Rather, God is looking for quality of worship.

Christianity is not a religion, per se; it is a person. It is Jesus Christ. It is a personal relationship with Jesus Christ. Worship is an intimate, expressive celebration, communication, at times a sobering conviction, but an overall beautiful relationship with God. Christian spirituality is an ongoing experiential journey of loving God through Christ Jesus our Lord. The journey begins with knowing we have a need. The need is God, and God is unknowable unless he grants us a revelation of himself which is found in Christ. Our first and basic need is to know the truth. Jesus Christ is our truth. The cross reveals to us that truth as God sees it. If one is not careful, one could easily miss it following our own ways. Jesus said, "God is spirit, and his worshipers must worship in spirit and in truth" (John 4:24). Jesus also said that God's word is truth. Therefore, it does bring us back to the study of the Word of God. Studying the Word of God and worship go hand-in-hand, as you really cannot do one without the other. Perhaps studying the Scripture is the highest form of worship. When one studies the Word, one begins to worship.

p. THE HEM OF HIS GARMENT

> *"And behold a woman . . .*
> *touched the hem of his garment."*
>
> —MATTHEW 9:20, KJV

This moving story of the woman touching the hem of the Lord's garment can also be found in Mark 5:28 and Luke 8:44. Why did she want to touch Him? Why does the emphasis seem to focus upon the hem of Christ's robe?

The hem is called a *tzitzit* in Hebrew. God commanded that these fringes on the corners of their garments be worn in obedience to him (Numbers 15:37–40). The *tzitzit* was to remind the Jews of all the commandments of the Lord. Jesus, being an observant Jew, would have worn them on the outside of his overgarment. This would have been like a heavy outer garment worn today by many Bedouins. The *tzitzit* was not merely a fringe decoration; rather, it was the most holy part of the garment.

Why would the woman be desirous to touch the hem or *tzitzit* of the Lord's outer garment? The prophet Malachi stated that "the Sun of righteousness [will] arise with healing in his wings" (Malachi 4:3, KJV). You see, the *tzitzit* (plural *tzitziyot*) were also referred to as wings. The woman obviously understood the prophecy and knew that if she could only touch the "wings" of his garment, she could be healed. This garment would also have been the Lord's prayer shawl as well as a garment used to keep warm at night and to keep the sun off by day.

Notice that she, being defiled by this disease, after touching the holy, was made whole. Understand that the prophet Haggai (2:11–13) made it very clear that if the unclean touches the clean, the clean shall become unclean. They feared that if the unholy would touch the holy, the holy would become defiled.

Oh, beloved, not so with Jesus! A few verses later, he even touched the dead body of the ruler's daughter and she rose from the dead. It was against the tradition of Judaism to touch the unclean, and yet the Lord took the dead girl's hand "and she arose."

The Lord does the impossible. He is the God of miracles. At times, he breaks all the tradition of men, for his ways are not our ways. He takes the unclean and makes them clean. He forgives our sins and casts them into the depths of the sea and remembers them no more. He spoke the worlds into existence. He walked on water and fed the multitudes. He rose from the dead and is coming again.

Jesus said, "Inasmuch as ye have done it unto one of the least of these my brethren, ye have done it unto me" (Matthew 25:40, KJV).

Lord, help me show Israel the "hem of [Your] garment" so they may touch you and be made whole.

q. THE LORD'S PRAYER

God said in Jeremiah 33:3, "Call to me, and I will answer you, and show you great and mighty things, which you do not know." I would like to share with you a few thoughts on prayer taken from Matthew chapter 6.

In the gospel of Luke, we are told that Jesus was praying in a certain place, and when he ceased, one of his disciples said to him, "Lord, teach us to pray."

In Matthew's account of this moment, we learn how to pray. This prayer is commonly called The Lord's Prayer or The Disciple's Prayer.

Success is found in faithfulness, holiness, integrity, in righteousness being obedient to God and his Word as we walk with him. Prayer is the key to that success. The importance of prayer cannot be overestimated. Martin Luther said, "To have prayed well is to have studied well." Let me add to his thought by saying, "To have prayed well is to have preached well, to have written well, to have worked well, to have resisted well, to have lived well, and to have died well." Let's look briefly at how to pray.

1. Pray authentically (Matthew 6:5).

The word "hypocrite" means "a play actor."

When you pray, do not act a part. Be sincere, be real, be vulnerable. Make-believe genuineness is impossible, for genuineness has to do with our inner reality. Genuineness is character that God sees, and there is no acting a part before God. God sees through all pretense and acting.

In prayer, be genuine, for you are dealing with God. Prayer is a personal transaction between the soul and God.

2. Pray in private (Matthew 6:6).

The idea is that everything and everybody is shut out except God and you.

You enter your prayer room and commune with God. The "room" has the idea of a place to store your valuables. The idea came from the wealthy storing there treasures in an inner chamber. You see, the place of real prayer is the Christian's treasure chamber. You are there in the midst of the treasures of Grace which God has given you, and it is in the inner chamber that God enriches the one who prays.

3. Pray specifically (Matthew 6:7–8).

To "use vain repetitions" is one Greek word that means primarily "to stammer." The one who stammers repeats his words in a meaningless way. The heathen pray this way and Jesus said, "[T]herefore do not be like them." The heathen think they must gain their god's attention and make an impression upon him in behalf of their petitions. Not so with God, for he knows what we have need of before we ask him! The asking is for our sakes, that our faith and love and hope may be exercised and strengthened.

4. Pray with community in mind (Matthew 6:9).

"Our Father in heaven..."

In this prayer (verses 9–13), "I," "me," and "my" do not appear. However, "we," "us," and "our" occur nine times. We are so united in the family of God in the sense of "family ties" that one cannot suffer without all suffering, and none of us can rejoice without all rejoicing. A blessing upon one is therefore a blessing upon all, and a curse upon one is a curse upon all.

5. Pray reverently (Matthew 6:9).

"Hallowed be your name..."

As God's children, we can cry "Abba Father," or Papa; however, we must not forget to be reverent. Let no word pass our lips which in any way takes the name of God in vain.

6. Pray with hope and anticipation (Matthew 6:10).

"Your kingdom come . . ."

Sometime soon, the King will return to set up his kingdom. It is our business to make ready for his return and to make him Lord and King of our lives. Christ is enthroned in every area of my being: intellectual, moral, spiritual, and physical. Crown him in the realm of faith, business, education, politics, and pleasure.

7. Pray submissively and aggressively (Matthew 6:10).

"Your will be done on earth as it is in heaven . . ."

Such is the standard we should have before us, and we should be satisfied with nothing less. This spirit will make us missionaries and send us with the Gospel to our world.

8. Pray dependently (Matthew 6:11).

"Give us this day our daily bread . . ."

"This day" refers to time. But the word "daily" has no thought of time. It means that something is needed or necessary. "Give us this day our needed sustenance to accomplish our tasks at hand."

9. Pray forgiving (Matthew 6:12).

"Forgive us our debts as we forgive our debtors."

We should forgive those who offend us or owe us just as God has forgiven us.

10. Pray cautiously (Matthew 6:13).

"Lead us not into temptation but deliver us from the evil one."

Believers recognize their spiritual weakness as they pray for deliverance from temptation to do evil. We would be wise not to battle without the Lord's protection. Do not battle in the flesh or in your own strength. The battle is the Lord's!

11. Doxology (Matthew 6:13).

"For yours is the kingdom and the power and the glory forever. Amen."

This doxology echoes 1 Chronicles 29:11, reminding us that all glory and power is the Lord's.

"Lord, teach us to pray" (Luke 11:1). We must make time to pray, for God works in answer to prayer. And "God at work" is our greatest need. Simply begin—work at it, trying different times of the day or night. Try again and again until it becomes part of your life.

> *"God does not tell you what he is going to do;
> he reveals to you who he is."*
>
> —Oswald Chambers, on prayer

Until he comes, we are together under his wings.

r. WALKING ON WATER

> *"Jesus made his disciples get into the boat and go before him to the other side, while he sent the multitudes away."*
>
> —Matthew 14:22

The Zealots

Five thousand people ate bountifully that day along the Sea. Galilee is where the Zealot movement, a revolutionary force that got Rome's attention, began. These revolutionaries formed about 30 years before the Lord began his ministry near Bethsaida, coming together around the time of the Incarnation.

Revolution

It was necessary for Jesus to dismiss this volatile crowd. In John's account, the crowd began to chant, "This is the Prophet who is to come . . ." (6:14–15). The crowd experienced the miracle and heard of Jesus' profound ministry and words regarding the Kingdom of Heaven; therefore, they began to believe he was the long-awaited Messiah. However, their idea of a messiah was a military / political redeemer. Jesus did not come to bring social order and political peace to the world at that time; peace and social order will come later. He came to redeem the lost and damaged souls of the human race. Blood—sacrificial blood—had to be spilled, not the blood that comes from a battlefield in a revolution.

This crowd would have been considered politically dangerous and word would have been sent to Herod Antipas about this crowd. The possible reaction by Rome would not have proven productive for Jesus or his followers. Two of the Lord's disciples (Simon the Zealot and Judas Iscariot) are believed to have belonged to the revolutionary movement and a special group within the movement called the Sicari assassins (one who would kill by using a small knife called a dagger).

Bird's-Eye View

Therefore, the Lord sent the disciples back out in the boat to get away from the crowd, and he himself vanished up the hills along the northern side of the lake. There he would often pray. From the hills (mountain), the Lord had a bird's eye view of the lake. Between prayers, the Lord could watch the disciples struggling with the oars and rudder (Mk. 6:48). The infamous *sharkiyeh* ("the east"), a cold east wind that happens in autumn of the year, kicked up and the boat was being tossed and turned around and around, side-to-side, water coming into the small boat as the disciples (mostly skilled fishermen) traded off rowing because of the exhaustion. This happened one time before in Matthew chapter 8, but this time Jesus was not in the boat with them. It seems as though the sea itself was trying to eradicate Jesus' key men. Jesus could see all of this unfolding from the high place of prayer. It seemed like hours, and certainly it was to the disciples who were struggling to survive.

What is That?

As the fishermen were to the point of complete exhaustion, watching the waves and swells go up and down and crashing into their tiny boat, they saw something in the dark early in the morning before sunrise. There is an object in the water . . . No, wait—it is on top of the water! It is a man! No, it is a ghost! (cf. Luke 24). What is that? "Lord is that really you?"

Jesus was walking on top of the waves, stepping over them like one who would step over rocks. He was not in the water, but on top of the waves and swells. He was about to walk past them.

"Do not be afraid," said Jesus. Then Jesus climbed into the boat (after Peter also walked on the water, of course). The storm ceased and the disciples worshiped him (literally prostrated themselves), saying, "Truly you are the Son of God."

History Begins to Divide

This is a major point in history. Judaism doesn't allow the worship of a man, no matter how religious he is. The disciples are beginning to understand there is something more profound about this one named Yeshua. He is more than a king or a political messiah. He is bigger than all these human expectations. Who is this man that walks on water? He is the Son of God, and soon they will understand that he is God in the flesh.

John's account of the story tells us that when they were willing to take him into the boat, they reached their destination on shore where they were heading (Jn. 6:21).

"He alone stretches out the heavens and treads on the waves of the sea. He is the Maker of the Bear and Orion, the Pleiades and the constellations of the south. He performs wonders that cannot be fathomed, miracles that cannot be counted. When he passes me, I cannot see him; when he goes by, I cannot perceive him."

—Job 9:8–11, NIV

Perhaps the disciples thought of Moses when Jesus said, "Do not be afraid, it is I." Moses said to Israel trapped in front of the Red Sea, "Do not be afraid. Stand firm and you will see the power of Yeshua (Jesus the Lord) . . . today" (Ex. 14:13).

Lessons Understood

1. Our hope does not rest with political movements. However, a believer can be a politician and be involved in politics in order to bring forth moral and ethical changes within government and society as a whole. However, Christianity must never be diminished to a political movement to defeat "Rome" for our convenience. Our faith in Christ encompasses a greater vision and hope for the entire world. He walks on water—it is bigger than us and our plans.

2. In the midst of the storm, though we cannot see him, God is watching and completely aware of our circumstances and knows what he will do for his followers, and his followers will see the effects of his presence at the right time.

3. To follow Christ does not mean we will avoid storms in our lives. Storms bring about change, and our understanding of God is never the same.
4. We will eventually arrive at our destination, and Christ will walk beside us to shore.
5. Recognizing the authority of the One who controls the Universe and creates all life, and know that he is also the One who sustains us with daily bread and all we need. He is worthy of our worship!

s. WHAT IS LOVE?

During the Last Supper, Jesus gathered his disciples and taught them a lesson they would never forget as he washed their feet. Throughout his ministry, the Lord would teach his "little children" many valuable lessons. On this final evening of his earthly ministry, the Lord gives them one final and perhaps his most powerful message. His message was simple, yet profoundly difficult: "Love as . . . I have loved you."

Love is a very unique commodity. Jesus fleshed out the perfect example of love, whether turning over the tables of the money changers, challenging the hypocrites, forgiving, or the ultimate sacrifice, giving his life for others.

Love doesn't put on a blindfold when it comes to discernment or depravity. Love deals very much with reality. Love is honest. Love is authentic. Love is unconditional and unselfish. Love is strong. Love is kind. Love is patient.

The Scripture is replete with references regarding love or God's love. As you read the Word of God, you find authentic love as manifested by our Lord Jesus Christ. May we be willing to yield to the Holy Spirit as he would move upon our hearts regarding this most important matter. When our friends, family, and community observe us, may they see the love of Christ within.

"A new commandment I give to you, that you love one another; as I have loved you, that you also love one another. By this all will know that you are my disciples, if you have love for one another."

—JOHN 13:34–35

t. WHO IS JESUS?

"Nathanael answered and saith unto him, 'Rabbi, thou art the Son of God; thou art the King of Israel.' Jesus answered and said unto him, 'Because I said unto thee, I saw thee under the fig tree, believest thou? Thou shalt see greater things than these.' And he saith unto him, 'Verily, verily, I say unto you, hereafter ye shall see heaven open, and the angels of God ascending and descending upon the Son of man.'"

—JOHN 1:49-51, KJV

Amen, Amen!

The word "amen" is a Hebrew word with roots in the ordinary Hebrew for belief, faithfulness, and truth. It is found closing the first book of Psalms: "Amen and amen" (Psalms 41:13). The double "amen" is used for solemn emphasis, to express the assurance that the prayer embodied in this doxology psalm would be answered. The same "amen, and amen" closes the second book of Psalms 72:19 and also the third book (Psalms 89:52). The fourth book ends with a single "amen," and then, "Praise ye the Lord" (Psalms 106:48). The final book of Psalms ends with five psalms, each beginning and ending with another great Hebrew word: "Hallelujah" ("Praise ye the Lord").

It is interesting that John records the word "amen" in the apocalypse as a name of Christ (Revelation 1:18, 3:14). It is the name by which he addressed himself to the lukewarm, end-time, Laodicean church. The word "amen" is also the last word in the Bible. The last thing God has to say to us is to leave us pondering a word that is a name for his beloved Son: "The grace of our Lord Jesus Christ be with you all. Amen" (Revelation 22:21, KJV).

Thus, grace and truth did indeed come by Jesus Christ and, after affirming that, God has no more to say. The double "amen" (translated "most assuredly" or "verily verily") is used to emphasize the Lord's divine authority to mark the importance of what he was about to say and to affirm the certainty of the truth he declared.

Ladders and Angels

The double "amen" got Nathanael's attention. It reminded him of Jacob's conversion and the ladder with the angels ascending and descending from heaven to earth. Jesus was saying to Nathanael, "I am the ladder that links heaven and earth, God and man. I am the way to heaven. You have called me the Son of God. I am! You have called me the King of Israel. I am! I am the only way to God. The angels ascend and descend in celebration of me."

Notice that the angels are ascending and descending, not descending and ascending. They are already here. They are stationed in every corner, every state, every country, everywhere people are located. Satan can't do anything about them. They are here for various reasons and they are in constant communication with Heaven's command.

There are guardian angels who watch over children. Jesus said, "Take heed that ye despise not one of these little ones; for I say unto you, that in heaven their angels do always behold the face of my Father which is in heaven" (Matthew 18:10). These angels ascend this glorious stairway, heavily burdened, reporting before a Holy God cases of child abuse, children who have been neglected, rejected, and aborted. Then they descend with their new orders from their commander and chief to care for the little ones assigned to them, to watch over and to protect and defend them.

There are angels who are assigned to God's own people, over churches. Some reports are not good. But, thankfully, there are good reports of faithfulness and revival. Do you ever wonder what they report about you?

King of Israel

"Son of man" has varying levels of emphasis, one of which is a title for the millennial kingdom in which the Son of man will sit on the throne in Jerusalem as King of Israel. There will be open communication between the heavenly Jerusalem and the earthly. Jesus is the glory of both.

"The title 'Son of man' appears twelve times in the Gospel of John . . . As the 'Son of man,' Jesus reveals divine truth (John 1:51); he has a supernatural origin (John 3:13, 6:62); his death by being 'lifted up' achieves salvation for men (John 3:14, 8:28, 12:34); he exercises the prerogative of final judgment (John 5:27); and he provides spiritual nourishment (John 6:27).

"This title is also used of his being glorified (John 12:23, 13:31), which John applies specifically to death and resurrection (John 7:39; 12:16) . . .

"In its general usage, it is the title of the incarnate Christ who is the representative of humanity before God and the representative of deity in human life. In the perfection of Christ's humanity, God finds the fullness of his expression to men."

"And he is before all things, and by him all things consist" (Colossians 1:17, KJV).

"For it pleased the Father that in him should all fullness dwell" (Colossians 1:19, KJV).

"For in him dwelleth all the fullness of the Godhead bodily. And ye are complete in him, which is the head of all principality and power" (Colossians 2:9–10, KJV).

". . . Christ is all, and in all" (Colossians 3:11b, KJV).

The Son of man, being Jacob's ladder, is God's link with earth.

"I saw in the night visions, and, behold, one like the Son of man came with the clouds of heaven, and came to the Ancient of days, and they brought him near before him" (Daniel 7:13, KJV).

"Jesus saith unto him, Thou hast said: nevertheless I say unto you, Hereafter shall ye see the Son of man sitting on the right hand of power, and coming in the clouds of heaven" (Matthew 26:64 KJV).

Are you connected with him? Do you believe? Are you traveling with him? Are you his disciple? Or are you still waffling in decision? Make a decision today.

Without Christ, you have no hope. He is our link to God, to eternal life.

What do you seek? What are you seeking? What are you seeking in life?

Jesus said, "Follow me," meaning "Come and travel with me. Come and journey with me." For Jesus is the Son of man. He is all and in all. He is all you need. You can be complete in him! He is our fortress and strength. He is life itself.

3

Encouragement

a. BEING IN CHRIST

IN EPHESIANS ALONE we find 40 references to being "in Christ" and having Christ in you. Being a Christian is not just a matter of getting something; it is a matter of being someone. A Christian is not simply a person who is forgiven and goes to Heaven. A Christian in terms of his or her deepest identity is a saint, a spiritually born child of God, a divine masterpiece, a child of light, and a citizen of heaven. Being born again transformed you into someone who didn't exist before. What you receive as a Christian isn't the point; it is who you are. It is not what you do as a Christian that determines who you are; it is who you are that determines what you do. One of the greatest ways to help yourself grow into maturity in Christ is to continually remind yourself who you are in him. The more you reaffirm who you are in Christ, the more your behavior will begin to reflect your true identity.

In Adam we die; however, we have been made a new creature with a new heart and spirit. In Christ we have become new, and all things are new and we have a new master. We are set apart in Christ. The greatest tension in the New Testament is between the indicative (what God has already done and what is already true about us) and the imperative (what remains to be done as we respond to God by faith and obedience in the power of the Holy Spirit).

To live under grace, we need to learn how to walk or live by the Spirit. The body of the spiritual person has also been transformed. It is now the dwelling place for the Holy Spirit and is being offered as a living sacrifice of worship and service to God. Walking by the Spirit is a relationship, not regimentation. Walking according to the Spirit is not license, nor is it legalism. Walking according to the Spirit implies two things. First, it is not sitting in the Spirit. Second, it is not running in the Spirit.

Every Christian is both a disciple and one who disciples in the context of his or her Christian relationships. It will take us the rest of our lives to renew our minds and to conform to the image of God.

b. CHANGE

"What God has cleansed you must not call common."

—Acts 11:9

Change? Me? Never!

Change is always a hard thing to accept. When Peter returned to Jerusalem after a revival among the Gentiles from Caesarea, he found that others were not as enthusiastic and supportive with this "good news." So Peter rehearsed the events in order to share with them what God was doing throughout the world.

It is very important for us as believers to understand what God is accomplishing throughout the world. Plus, we must differentiate between things that are absolute and non-absolute. The absolutes are factors like historic doctrines and foundations for faith and practice. The non-absolutes are matters relating to style and methodology that are subject to upgrading and updating.

We need to be open vessels, allowing God to bring about change in our lives for his honor and glory. What are you holding back from God? He will not force himself upon you; rather, he will gently woo you through his Spirit.

Is God speaking to your heart? Are you at a point of decision? Trust him and let him do what is pleasing in his sight.

"Call to me, and I will answer you
and show you great and mighty things, which you do not know."

—Jeremiah 33:3

c. COMMUNITY

The Bible is written in the context of Israel or the church community. Believers belong together. That is the way God made us, and that's the way God deals with us. In the Old Testament, God called Abraham to follow him—not just so God could bless Abraham, but his descendants also. Yes, there were people like Moses, Elijah, Jeremiah, Esther, and Deborah. However, they operated within the framework of God's chosen nation, Israel.

Jesus did the same thing. He didn't work alone, but chose an inner circle of 12 followers to learn from him and to get the message out. After he left and the Spirit came and this little group began to grow, the church was born.

In the early church, it was wonderful and amazing as they discovered that all Christians had something in common: They had the same Holy Spirit that lived in each person. They discovered they had the same goals and desires and gifts that the Holy Spirit gave to each of them. You can travel around the world, and when you come across another Christian, there is a bond. You are of the same family with the same goals and desires and gifts no matter what your background.

In Christ we are one. We worship together. We come together to praise and thank God for what he has done. We bring our needs to him. We listen to what he has to say. We remember what he has done for us and we reaffirm our faith. We remind ourselves that he is Lord and we must become content with God alone.

d. DO I FEAR GOD?

"Then Joseph said to them the third day,
"Do this and live, for I fear God."'

—GENESIS 42:18

On this day, ask yourself:
"Do I fear God?"
"Am I honest?"
"Am I setting a godly example for others to see?"
"Do I love the Lord with all my heart, soul, mind, and strength?"
"Do others see Christ in me?"

Thomas A. Kempis stated in *The Imitation of Christ* (chapter 3, paragraph 3), "O God, living Truth, unite me to yourself in everlasting love! Often I am wearied by all I read and hear. In you alone is all that I desire and long for. Therefore, let all teachers keep silence, and let all creation be still before you: You, O Lord, speak alone."

As you mine the riches of God's Word, may your heart rejoice in God's provision for his children and the hope that only comes through God's redeeming grace through Jesus Christ our Lord.

God is sovereign! God is holy! He will see to it!

e. DON'T BE AFRAID

Economic Problems & Natural Disasters
Problems and Solutions from the Prophet Haggai

With the Babylonian exile in the past and Jews returning to the land, the work of rebuilding the Temple began. However, the project was pushed aside as a result of putting personal affairs first. Things began to happen to the nation. Economic problems unfolded and natural disasters began to happen. Let's find out what happened some 2,500 years ago.

Problem: Financial

The Lord said, "Give careful thought to your ways. You have planted much, but have harvested little. You eat, but never have enough. You drink, but never have your fill. You put on clothes, but are not warm. You earn wages, only to put them in a purse with holes in it" (Hag. 1:5–6, NIV).

Solution: Do What is Right: Put the Lord First

"'Give careful thought to your ways . . . so that I may take pleasure in it and be honored,' says the Lord." (Hag. 1:7–8, NIV)

Problem: Natural Disasters

"You expected much, but see, it turned out to be little. What you brought home, I blew away. Why? declares the Lord Almighty. Because of my house, which remains a ruin, while each of you is busy with his own house. Therefore, because of you the heavens have withheld their dew and the earth its crops. I called for a drought on the fields and the mountains, on the grain, the new wine, the oil and whatever the ground produces, on men and cattle, and on the labor of your hands." (Hag. 1:9–11, NIV)

Solution: Obedience

"The people obeyed the voice of the Lord their God and the message of the prophet Haggai . . . and the people feared the Lord . . . 'I am with you,' declares the Lord." (Hag. 1:12–13, NIV)

Problem: Doesn't Look the Same

"Who of you is left who saw this house in its former glory? How does it look to you now? Does it not seem to you like nothing?" (Hag. 2:3, NIV)

Solution: Be Strong in the Lord

"Be strong . . . Be strong . . . Be strong . . . for I am with you, declares the Lord . . . My Spirit remains among you. Do not fear." (Hag. 2:4–5, NIV)

All of It Belongs to the Lord!

"'The silver is mine and gold is mine,' declares the Lord . . . 'And in this place I will grant peace . . .'" (Hag. 2:6–9, NIV)

Never Forget

"Give careful thought . . . from this day on—consider how things were before one stone was laid . . . you did not turn to me . . . but (because of your repentance) from this day on I will bless you . . ." (Hag. 2:15–19, NIV)

Nothing is new! Because of selfishness, sin, and pride, disasters both economic and natural fell upon Israel. Only when they repented, changed their ways, and trusted in the Lord did these calamities change. There were still scars; it didn't look the same. Nevertheless, God was with them and he said to them, "Never forget what happened, where you came from and what I did for you! I own it all; therefore, bow before me and do what is right!" Don't be afraid; God owns it all. Trust in him and be obedient to his Word.

f. GOD'S NAVEL

"Who dwell in the midst of the land . . ."

—Ezekiel 38:12

Did you ever want to part of something bigger than yourself? Ever want to do something profound? Do you want to be remembered as a person who made a difference?

"In the midst of the land" literally means "in the navel or center of the world." The prophet is saying that Israel is the center of the world, the center of all things important. He is absolutely correct!

To understand what God is doing in the world, we must ask ourselves, "What is God doing in Israel?" Beloved, when you bless Israel, you are blessing God's plan for his ancient people Israel. You become part of prophecy in the last days.

When you bless God's ancient people, you are taking part in something bigger than yourself; you are touching the "apple of God's eye" (Zechariah 2:8).

Not only when you bless the seed of Abraham will you be blessed, but when you touch anyone in Christ's name it is as though you are blessing Jesus himself. "Inasmuch as you did it to one of the least of these, my brethren, you did it to me" (Matt. 25:40).

So get out there and go to the center of the world, into God's navel, and bless someone in the name of Jesus. You will receive much greater joy than if you do nothing! And you will be making a difference in the world.

g. HE MADE THE STARS ALSO

Genesis 1:16

What an awesome thought to ponder as you consider the billions of stars that exist. These five words reflect the sovereign creative ability of God (Hebrew *Elohim*, making reference to His majestic power). The phrase "he made the stars also" is like an afterthought. "Oh, by the way, God (*Elohim*) created the stars also." Wow!

From time to time, we need to be reminded that God is sovereign and has a plan for the universe and specifically your life. The prophet

Isaiah reminds us, "Thus saith God the Lord, he that created the heavens, and stretched them out; he that spread forth the earth, and that which cometh out of it; he that giveth breath unto the people upon it, and spirit to them that walk therein: I, the Lord have called thee in righteousness, and will hold thine hand, and will keep thee..." (Isaiah 42:5–6, KJV).

We can see in these verses that God has great concern and truly cares for his people. If God can create "the stars also" in all their glory and magnificence, can he not care for your concerns and needs? Listen to the words of David as he asks, "What is man, that thou art mindful of him? And the son of man, that thou visitest him? For thou hast made him a little lower than the angels, and hast crowned him with glory and honor" (Psalm 8:4–5, KJV).

The term "mindful" suggests that God is continually thinking about man. We are constantly on his mind. He has crowned those who trust in him with glory and honor. One day, believers in Jesus will be his trophies of grace, eternally displayed before all creation (Ephesians 2:7). Also, David states, with extreme pathos, "I am poor and needy; yet the Lord thinketh upon me: Thou art my help and my deliverer; make no tarrying, O my God" (Psalm 40:17, KJV).

The word "thinketh" (thinks) has the idea "to regard and value"— just as the parent or grandparent that carries around photos of their children or grandchildren, ready to show them at any moment. In the back of their mind, they are constantly cherishing and regarding their kids or grandkids. So it is with God and his children—he thinks upon us.

Be not afraid, dear one, "for in him we live and move and have our being." The Lord Jesus will never leave us nor forsake us. We are "complete in Him" who is "all and in all" (Acts 17:28; Hebrews 13:5; Colossians 2:10, 3:11).

Therefore, rest in the confidence that he who "made the stars also" can complete that which he has started in you and will hold your hand and keep you along the journey. Amen and amen!

h. IMPORTANCE OF LIFE

"I have come that they may have life."

—John 10:10

We have been given a great gift: the gift of life.

"And the Lord God formed man of the dust of the ground and breathed into his nostrils the breath of life; and man became a living soul" (Genesis 2:7, KJV).

By virtue of this act, man has been given a special relationship with his Creator. For it was man, not the animals, who had the breath of life blown into his nostrils by God himself. By this direct act did man become a living being, drawing directly from God his source of life. On Mars Hill in Athens, Paul stated that God "gives to all life, breath . . . for in him we live and move and have our being" (Acts 17:25–28, KJV).

We are different from the beasts of the field. This is quite obvious due to the fact that beasts react instinctively while humans express intellect, and free will, having an awareness of their own existence and a degree of self-control. Therefore, human life is precious and has purpose. David writes, "For I am fearfully and wonderfully made . . . How precious also are thy thoughts unto me" (Psalm 139:14, 17, KJV).

Always remember that you are here at this hour, this minute, this second, in this universe, on this planet for a reason. You are no mistake—God makes no mistakes!

Human life is precious. We understand this in light of Scripture. I am reminded of our Lord's teaching in Luke chapter 15 regarding the one lost sheep and the one lost coin and the one lost boy. It is from Jesus that we learn that each person is precious in the sight of God. Within each human being, there is dignity and a soul made in the image of God, and for those who trust in Christ, their very body is the temple of the Holy Spirit from Heaven. To each one, God has placed the light of intelligence. You are precious in God's sight, and there is meaning and purpose for your life.

The Apostle John tells us in John 1:3–4 that Jesus is the very essence of life. Jesus is God, and those who trust in him alone as Savior will spend eternity in the presence of God who is the source of all life. Jesus said, "I am the way, the truth, and the life; no one comes to the Father except through me" (John 14:6).

John also stated in John 3:36 that "[h]e who believes in the Son has everlasting life; and he who does not believe the Son shall not see life, but the wrath of God abides on him." Jesus declares that "[h]e who believes in him is not condemned" (John 3:18).

Your life is so precious that Jesus died on Calvary's cross for your sins. This is why he came, for those who reject him will spend eternity without him in a Christ-less Hell. However, those who believe in Christ alone will receive the gift of eternal life and experience the splendor of Heaven.

You are precious in God's sight. Make your life complete by trusting in Christ as Lord and Savior.

l. IT DOES MATTER!

"Now when they had come and gathered the church together, they reported all that God had done . . . and that he had opened the door of faith . . ."

—ACTS 14:27

After their first missionary journey, Paul and Barnabas reported to the church at Antioch what great things God had done. With great enthusiasm and thanksgiving, they shared story after story. Indeed, we also have much to share with thanksgiving. Allow me to list a few blessings that define mature Christians:

1. A Loving Spirit

    Love does matter. Jesus said, "By this all will know that you are my disciples, if you have love for one another" (John 13:35).

2. A Growing Unity

    Working together to flesh out the Great Commission. Unity does matter. Jesus also said, "That they all may be one . . . that the world may believe . . ." (John 17:21)

3. Commitment to the Word

    An insatiable hunger for the teaching of the Word of God within the church is a very healthy sign. Truth does matter. For the disciples "continued steadfastly in the apostles' doctrine . . ." (Acts 2:42)

4. Celebrated Community

   There is a growing desire to fellowship with one another. Community does matter. "If you don't care about loving the Church, you don't care too much about her founder!" The disciples "continued . . . in . . . fellowship . . . all who believed were together . . ." (Acts 2:42, 44)

5. Love for God

   It is becoming evident that you love the Lord God with all your heart, soul, mind, and with all your strength (Deuteronomy 6:5). Love for God does matter.

6. Love for Humanity

   Your testimony is strong and sure. You are reaching out beyond our four walls. You are moving forward for the cause of Christ as precious souls are being blessed in the name of Jesus. Love for people does matter. "And the Lord added to the church daily those who were being saved" (Acts 2:47).

7. A Growing Awareness of Missions

   A love for missions is developing in your life. This is indeed the heartbeat of Christ's church. World evangelism does matter. "Go into all the world and preach the gospel to every creature" (Mark 16:15).

God is so faithful to his children and he loves us more than we can fathom. Our lives belong to him. We need to remember that we are leaving a legacy for our children, grandchildren, and great-grandchildren. May we be found faithful following Christ, his Word, and his will for our lives until he comes for us.

How can we remain faithful?

1. Pray
2. Study the Word
3. Fellowship with one another
4. Share your faith with others
5. Be generous in giving.
6. Get involved with other lives—become salt and light.

J. MUSIC

"Finally, brethren, whatsoever things are true, whatsoever things are honest, whatsoever things are just, whatsoever things are pure, whatsoever things are lovely, whatsoever things are of good report; if there be any virtue, and if there be any praise, think on these things."

—Phil. 4:8, KJV

All good things do come from God. The Scripture never condemns good music, literature, or art. David played and listened to music. His psalms were put to music. Jesus sang songs and participated in the cultural arts and festivals of the first century. If music, literature, or art condemns God, promoting destructive or hellish activity, encouraging that which stands in antithesis to purity and godliness, then turn away from such.

Christians should be involved in the arts. We should appreciate the various styles of architecture, the diverse motifs in art, and the wonder of rhapsody, sonata, and opera, as well as country, gospel, hymns, and contemporary forms of music.

If we reject all knowledge but religious knowledge, if we ignore all music but Christian music, if we renounce all literature but sacred literature, if we repudiate all art except church art, then we as Christians fail to understand that all good creativity comes from God.

If Christians would become involved, the arts, sciences, and all the humanities could become a reflection of Christ for his glory, bringing all men to an awareness of himself.

One final thought regarding music in the words of Martin Luther: "The devil should not be allowed to keep all the best tunes for himself. I have no use for cranks who despise music, because it is a gift of God. Next after theology, I have music the highest place and greatest honor."

"Whatsoever ye do, do all to the glory of God."

—1 Cor. 10:31, KJV

k. NO SHORTCUTS

*"But as for you, you meant evil against me,
but God meant it for good . . ."*

—Genesis 50:20

A man found a cocoon of the emperor moth and took it home to watch it emerge. One day, a small opening appeared, and for several hours the moth struggled but couldn't seem to force its body past a certain point.

Deciding something was wrong, the man took scissors and snipped the remaining bit of cocoon. The moth emerged easily, its body large and swollen, the wings small and shriveled.

He expected that in a few hours the wings would spread out in their natural beauty, but they did not. Instead of developing into a creature free to fly, the moth spent its life dragging around a swollen body and shriveled wings.

The constricting cocoon and the struggle necessary to pass through the tiny opening are God's way of forcing fluid from the body into the wings. The "merciful" snip was, in reality, cruel. Sometimes the struggle is exactly what we need.

May we learn some basic principles regarding our need to depend on God and not on our flesh.

In times of trial and testing, seek the face of God and he will find you.

l. REGARDING UNANIMITY

1. Unanimity is the goal and consists of understanding the "whole picture," a "Christian worldview," or "space-shuttle view." This involves the understanding of differentiation between preference and biblical principle. You may prefer a certain style or method, but is it consistent with the biblical principal?
2. The "majority" doesn't necessarily mean God's will (Numbers 11).
3. A perfect example is found in Acts 15, where the disciples arrived at a unanimous consensus regarding a most controversial issue.

In John 17, the Lord's concern for his disciples was their unity, not their uniformity. He recognized they were different from one another. The Lord cherished the fact they had diversity.

At times, in our passion to do what is right according to scripture or to help others conform to Christ's image, we forget that God doesn't make photocopies of us. He uses our uniqueness in his ultimate plan. One is a detail person; another is a visionary; one is a helper; another can manage; others can orchestrate. God uses everyone for his purposes. We are all doing life together—we all need each other.

Therefore, if others are not doing things exactly your way, chill out—it's okay! God is in control! Never forget it is the Lord who owns it all, not you.

Thus, unanimity is not uniformity.

m. YES, JESUS LOVES ME!

> *"This is my commandment: that you love one another as I have loved you."*
>
> —JOHN 15:12

As Jesus leads his disciples through the winding paths of the beautiful Kidron Valley, they walk through vineyards and olive groves to the base of the Mount of Olives. From there, the Lord will lead them to Gethsemane.

Before the fateful moment of prayer and betrayal, the Lord gives his bewildered band a few final words to ponder: "[L]ove one another as I have loved you."

It must sadden our Lord when his children complain or criticize one another. Sometimes we fail to love unconditionally. Jesus said, " [L]ove . . . as I have loved you."

The way the Lord loved his disciples reminds us how he loves us, for he loved them unconditionally . . .

1. In their unbelief (Matthew 14:31).
2. In their small-mindedness (John 18:1–6).
3. In their desertion (John 26:31).

4. In their denial (John 26:33-34).
5. In their laziness (John 26:36-46).
6. In their betrayal (John 26:47-50).
7. To the end (John 13:1).

Lord, may I love others as you love me!

4

Hebraic Thoughts

a. THE SCRIPTURES JESUS READ AND ORIGEN, AN EARLY CHURCH FATHER

PEOPLE FORGET THAT THE scripture texts that Jesus read and referred to when he spoke were the Hebrew Scriptures, commonly called the Old Testament by Christians. One must realize that there is nothing "old" about them. Scripture is always relevant and never out of date or not applicable.

Heretic

Marcion, a second-century heretic who died around 160 AD, emphasized the insignificance of the Old Testament and endeavored to sever the Jewish connection of New Testament Christianity. Origen of Alexandria (185–254 AD) worked diligently to repair the damage done by Marcion a few decades later.

Pastor's Heart

Origen had a pastor's heart and desired to see people come to faith in Jesus the Messiah. There are many commentaries in existence today written by Origen covering Old Testament books. As with any early Christian writings you will find strengths, weaknesses, and some controversy.

Beheaded

The eldest of seven siblings born to Christian parents, Origen learned what it meant to be a believer in Jesus. His father, Leonides, was beheaded for being a Christian in 202 AD, during the nefarious Emperor Septimus Severus's rule. After Leonides's execution, all of his family's possessions were stolen by the authorities.

Teacher

Origen became a teacher in both secular and religious realms. Eventually, he sold his library for very little money and dedicated his life to the teaching of Christian principals, preaching the gospel, and living a life of self-denial. He lived throughout the Mediterranean, spending most of his time in the Middle East.

Guidelines

Origen did not try to "Hellenize" (Greek cultural emphasis) his writings; rather, he endeavored to interpret the Old Testament Scripture using the guidelines of Jesus, Paul, and other New Testament writers. Because of this, I find his body of work fascinating.

According to *Ancient Christian Texts, Homilies on Numbers, Origen* (IVP Academic, Intervarsity Press, 2009, p. xxviii), Origen tells his hearers to go back to the Gospels and Paul in order to find examples of "spiritual interpretation" regarding the Old Testament texts. He was influenced by the famous Philo of Alexandria and a friend who was a Jewish believer in Yeshua (Jesus) and whose father was a rabbi. Though his Jewish friend taught him rabbinical principles of how to interpret the Scriptures, Origen chose the pattern of interpretation found in the New Testament itself. Below are the texts for Origen's hermeneutics (how to interpret Scripture):

- Hebrews 10:1: "The law is only a shadow of the good things that are coming—not the realities themselves . . ." (NIV)
- 1 Corinthians 10:11: "Now all these things happened to them as examples, and they were written for our admonition, upon whom the ends of the ages have come." (NKJV)
- Romans 15:4: "For everything that was written in the past was written to teach us, so that through endurance and the encouragement of the Scriptures we might have hope." (NIV)
- 2 Timothy 3:16,17: "All Scripture is given by inspiration of God, and is profitable for doctrine, for reproof, for correction, for instruction in righteousness, that the man of God may be complete, thoroughly equipped for every good work." (NKJV)

Therefore, Origen asks, "In light of St. Paul's claims about the Old Testament in these passages, what foreshadowing, what warning, what instruction, what encouragement, reproof, correction, or exhortation do we find in the narratives?"

Find Personal Meaning

Origen strived to find the literal, historical, mystical, and symbolic application of the Hebrew Scriptures. Oftentimes, Origen would encourage his hearers to conduct their own inductive study of the Bible to find personal meaning.

Very simply, imitating the study methods of the Apostle Paul is a great way to study Old Testament scripture. We must never forget that the Old Testament is for the church. May those who read and teach the Bible include the brilliant discovery of the first 39 books! One will not completely comprehend nor appreciate the New Covenant (New Testament) without knowing the First Covenant (Old Testament) from God.

It is good to have teachers like Origen who teach the whole council of God. May the Lord raise up an army of leaders who are thoroughly equipped for teaching the scriptures Jesus read in union with the continuing narrative of Scripture regarding the life, teachings, and meaning of Jesus the Messiah! Why? Time is short, life is precious, and Jesus is coming soon . . .

b. BLESSING

"I will bless them that bless thee."

—Genesis 12:3, KJV

Jewish life is replete with *berakhot*, or blessings. There are blessings for food and wine. There are blessings for smelling fragrant oils, fruits, and plants. There are blessings for sight and hearing and so forth.

Perhaps the most intriguing blessing is the *Birkat Kohanim*, or the "Priestly Blessing," sometimes called "Aaron's Blessing": "The Lord bless thee, and keep thee: The Lord make his face shine upon thee, and be gracious unto thee: The Lord lift up his countenance upon thee, and give thee peace" (Numbers 6:24–26, KJV).

The blessing was recited daily by the priests. They would ascend to a special platform, cover their heads, and with outstretched arms recite the ancient blessing.

The blessing starts with petition for material blessing, then spiritual blessing, and finally the greatest blessing of all: Shalom—peace.

The blessing points the pilgrim to a personal encounter with God. This is the only way to find true peace. The Lord Jesus became the "Passover Lamb," the atonement for sin. The prophet stated that the Messiah "was wounded for our transgressions, he was bruised for our iniquities: the chastisement of our peace was upon him; and with his stripes we are healed" (Isaiah 53:5, KJV).

As a result of the cross, you and I can have a personal encounter with God through the shed blood of the Messiah, the Lord Jesus, by trusting in him alone for salvation.

Jesus said he was the Messiah, and his life, death, and resurrection was proof. It is only through the Messiah, the Lord Jesus, that you and I can fully understand and experience Aaron's Blessing in finding true provision, purpose, and peace.

c. CHRISTIAN-ESE

Did you know that the first day of each Jewish month is known as Rosh *Chodesh*? Jewish months may have 29 or 30 days. When there are 30 days, two days are celebrated: the last (thirtieth) day of the previous month and the first day of the new month. When there are 29 days in the month, the first day of the new month is celebrated. This is the first day of the new moon.

Jewish months are based on the lunar calendar. Numbers 28:11 states, "And in the beginnings of your months ye shall offer a burnt offering unto the Lord." This holiday is considered a minor holiday or festival. Special blessings and psalms are recited, and the reading of Numbers 28:1–15 are part of the observance.

In my opinion, the most important point is that it is a time of reflection on the past month and a pondering how one can do better in the new month.

With Rosh *Chodesh* in mind, may our hearts reflect on the blessings of God that came upon our lives. Let us be encouraged to serve the Lord with all our heart, soul, mind, and strength in the coming year. Offer the Lord a sacrifice of praise and put into action our words of faith.

May we try to love more, share more, give more, bless our neighbors by doing a good deed for them, forgive, pray more—simply do rather than talk our "Christian-ese" (you know—it's like Chinese or Japanese: Christian-ese). May Christ find us even more committed to him, being like him in our deeds in the days ahead!

d. HALAKAH: WALKING THE WALK

"He hath shewed thee, O man, what is good; and what doth the Lord require of thee, but to do justly, and to love mercy, and to walk humbly with thy God."

—MICAH 6:8, KJV

This verse reflects what some call the "Jewish Golden Rule" and is termed Halakah. Halakah is the quintessential characteristic of Judaism[1]. The word Halakah is derived from the Hebrew word for "walking." Not only is Halakah the legal part of the Talmud, it is the way a religious Jew lives out his faith. By following rules of conduct as described in the Bible, as interpreted by the rabbis (i.e., the Ten Commandments, circumcision, keeping Shabbat, keeping kosher, etc.), religious Jews believe the "Holy One" will be pleased and accept them eternally. In essence, the Halakah is the path that the Jew must follow throughout his life[2]. Halakah has been the instrument by which Judaism has expressed its theology and morality[3].

The early church reflected this concept of Halakah. For example, the Apostle John wrote, "He that saith he abideth in him ought himself also so to walk, even as he walked" (1 John 2:6, KJV). Also, Paul wrote to the Ephesians explaining how the Christian ought to walk in chapters 4, 5, and 6. He addresses unity, compassion, holiness, truthfulness, obedience, and so on. In one chapter, he writes, "Be ye therefore followers (or imitators) of God . . . and walk in love, as Christ also hath loved us . . ." (Ephesians 5:1-2, KJV) Eight times in Ephesians, Paul uses the word "walk," which means "to walk around" or "to order one's behavior." This is the idea of Halakah.

Early church fathers also understood Halakah. Polycarp, a disciple of the Apostle John, wrote that ". . . we must gird on the armor of integrity, and the first step must be to school our own selves into conformity with the Divine commandments."[4] In the first century, Ignatius of Antioch declared, ". . . do not have Jesus Christ on your lips, and the world in your heart."5 In reference to the Christian's lifestyle, Francis of Assisi in the early thirteenth century stated, "Preach the gospel at all times. If necessary, use words."

We find in Romans 11:11 that ". . . salvation is come unto the Gentiles, for to provoke them (the Jews) to jealousy." The natural question would be, "What would cause them to be jealous?" First of all, anyone, Jew or Gentile, would be jealous of

1. The security that comes from the hope and peace a believer has in Jesus (Romans 5:1–11).
2. The love that is manifested between those who believe (Galatians 5:22–23).
3. Life—your life, your Halakah, will speak louder than any words you say.

"Walking the walk" will provoke both Jew and Gentile to jealousy. As one dear Jewish man stated, "I've read the New Testament and I like the Jesus of the Gospels . . . however, I do not like the Jesus I see in the churches." My dear Christian reader, what are we showing those around us? Are we "walking the walk" (Halakah) or are we simply talking a good talk? May God help us to imitate the "Jesus of the Gospels" in our lives.

Endnotes

1. Sigal, Philip. *Judaism: The Evolution of a Faith.* Grand Rapids: Eerdmans, 1988.
2. Himelstein, Rabbi Dr. Shmuel. *The Jewish Primer: Questions and Answers on the Jewish Faith and Culture.* Facts on File The Jerusalem Publishing House, 1990.
3. Sigal, Philip. *Judaism: The Evolution of a Faith.* Grand Rapids: Eerdmans, 1988.
4. Staniforth, Maxwell. *Early Christian Writings: The Apostolic Fathers.* Penguin Books, 1984.
5. Ibid.

e. ISAAC WAS COMFORTED

"And Isaac brought her into his mother Sarah's tent, and took Rebekah, and she became his wife; and he loved her: and Isaac was comforted after his mother's death."

—Genesis 24:67, KJV

This is a peculiar verse. What does it mean—"Isaac was comforted after his mother's death"? What void did Rebekah fill? What was so significant in this event that caused the Holy Spirit to guide Moses to record this vignette of Isaac's life?

To understand this verse is to understand the role of the woman in Jewish culture. God said concerning Adam, "It is not good that the man should be alone: I will make him a help meet for him" (Genesis 2:18, KJV). The emphasis here is that "[i]t is NOT good," this lonesomeness of man. Therefore, "I will make him a help meet," meaning "one who rescues."

The woman plays a most important role in the Jewish home, especially with regard to the Sabbath day observance. Sabbath—or Shabbat—is the holiest day of the week. It is the time between the sun setting on Friday evening and the sun setting on Saturday eve. It is a time of worship, scripture reading, prayer, a special meal, special bread, the lighting of candles, rest, remembering the Creator and his creation, and a celebration of life. The Jewish people are exhorted to "[r]emember the Sabbath day, to keep it holy" (Exodus 20:8, KJV).

Sarah, Isaac's mother, had passed away and left a huge void in the life of the family. When she was alive, her presence nurtured a reminder of the blessings of God. As the one who rescues, she would light the candles each Shabbat. She would prepare the *challah* dough, the rising dough, the "miraculous increase" of the special bread. From the lit candles—which are symbols of hope—from the light she created, a cloud would form that hovered in, throughout, and over the tent. Passersby would notice the hazy cloud. The delicate scent of the candle would kiss the senses of anyone near its glow. The tent itself was an insignia of provision and safety.

Understanding these truths, we are reminded that the weekly tasks Sarah performed were wonderfully symbolic. They pointed to the great hope that one day Messiah will come and bring redemption. That messianic anticipation pulsated within the veins of Jewish belief. This profound hope is pronounced clearly within the Scriptures.

The Light

The light of the candle represents the light of God. When the Menorah (the seven branch candle in the Temple) was lit, it is said that the light emanating from its golden lamp dispelled the darkness and shadows from all the corners of the Temple, and from there throughout the whole world. Sarah's act of lighting the candles leads us to the truth that the light of God's love dispels the darkness of sin and brings hope to the recipient. Jesus said it this way: "I am the light of the world: he that followeth me shall not walk in darkness, but shall have the light of life" (John 8:12, KJV).

Jesus, the Messiah, shed his blood on cruel Roman cross. He became our sin offering, our Passover lamb, so that anyone who believes in Him will be redeemed, receiving eternal life. Without the shedding of blood, there is no forgiveness of sin (Hebrews 9:22).

The light within Sarah's tent is a type of Jesus the Messiah, who is the Light that dispels the darkness of sin in the heart of man, for those who receive Jesus as Savior will experience hope, life, joy, forgiveness, and light (John 1:1–17).

The Bread

The *challah* bread reminds us of the provision of God. "Give us this day our daily bread." Bread and water are the main staples in the wilderness. Christians are pilgrims just passing through the wilderness of this life.

Our lives speak volumes as to who we are. We belong to the Most High God. We are in this world; however, we are not of the world. We live, work, and interact within the construct of this world and its social system. Christians are salt and light in their community. Believers must embrace life with a passion, as life is a gift from God. We must never be hesitant to experience the fullness of humanity, as we are created in God's image. Therefore, as Christians, we must move forward in our journey, knowing that the Lord is with us and that he will never leave us without provision.

Every morning, the Israelites found manna from God, the bread from heaven. Likewise, we must daily make the journey and search for those delightful treasures that God has provided, tailored just for us. You will discover hope, joy, peace, goodness, compassion, and mercy, to name a few blessings of God's provision.

God's grace is always evident throughout our "pilgrim's progress." Even when we walk through the valleys of testing, trial, and sorrow, we find wonderful treasures. We discover the golden nuggets of God's provision, the sweet smell and taste of the warm and sweet, miraculously increasing, never-ending bread of God's grace and mercy.

The *challah* (twisted bread) that Sarah baked was symbolic of God's watchful provision in the wilderness. It is a common bread like the bread at Pentecost (Hebrew *Shavuot*). All are welcome. As she kneaded the dough, we are reminded of that we are clay in the Master's hand. The sweet smell of rising dough causes us to remember that Jesus has given himself for us as a sweet, fragrant offering and sacrifice to God (Ephesians 5:2).

When Abraham and Isaac entered the tent where Sarah was baking the bread, they were brought face to face with the hope of the Messiah, the Anointed One, the Bread of Life. One day he will come. In fact, he did!

Jesus, our Lord and Savior, is our "bread." He is the Bread of Life. He is our sustenance. Without him, we can do nothing (John 15:5). He is the living Word; therefore, we are sustained by learning from him (Matthew 11:29; John 1:1, 14).

We learn from him by reading the Scriptures. Jesus said, "I am the bread of life: he that cometh to me shall never hunger; and he that believeth on me shall never thirst" (John 6:35, KJV).

Sarah was doing more than just baking bread; she was showing us "the Way, the Truth and the Life" (John 14:6).

The Cloud

The cloud that the candle produced that hovered in, throughout, and above the tent reminds us of God's presence. The cloud is symbolic of the *Shechinah* glory that was present in the wilderness in the form of a cloud. It was also present in the Tabernacle and Temple. The cloud also appeared on the Mount of Transfiguration. It represents God's glory.

The presence of the cloud reminded those near its splendor, awe, and terror that God is holy and to be reverenced. People knew that God was worshipped and was present when they walked by Sarah's tent. There is something different about people when they worship God. There is clear evidence that a person has placed their faith and trust in the Lord Jesus as they become a new creature (2 Corinthians 5:17). There is something unique and wonderful about those who believe in God. The glory that Jesus had with the Father before the world was has been given to those who believe in him (John 17:5, 22). It will be clear to all that you are a child of God. The glory of God will be upon you. Passersby will know you are a follower of God.

The Tent

When we think of the tent, we think of the Tabernacle—sometimes called the "tent of meeting"—the place where the Israelites and all the people were called to meet God. The tabernacle or tent was patterned after the heavenly tabernacle (Hebrews 8:2, 9:11; Revelation 13:6, 15:5, 21:3). Subsequently, we are reminded of the eternal, where God dwells and where the saints abide. The tent was a place of activity, responsibility, and service.

The tent was also symbolic of the relationship between husband and wife. God told Moses to have the men return to their tents, meaning to go back to their wives (Deuteronomy 5:30, 20:7). Paul taught that the relationship between husband and wife represents the mystical, mysterious, and miraculous union between the church and Messiah (Ephesians 5:22–33). Believers in Jesus are one with God. Jesus is God!

Rebekah

Rebekah (Hebrew *Rivkah*) brought joy, brightness, hope, life, and a renewed faith as the spirit of God dwelled in her. Isaac was comforted by her presence mentally, emotionally, physically, and spiritually. This is true of anyone who believes in Messiah Jesus. Jesus said, "I am come that they might have life, and that they might have it more abundantly" (John 10:10, KJV).

The Lord brings peace, joy, life, fullness, purpose, provision, protection, and comfort. We are complete in him (Colossians 2:10), and through him we will find totality of life in the human experience and in the eternal hope.

Jesus said, "Come unto me, all ye that labor and are heavy laden, and I will give you rest. Take my yoke upon you, and learn of me; for I am meek and lowly in heart: and ye shall find rest unto your souls. For my yoke is easy, and my burden is light" (Matthew 11:28–30, KJV).

f. JESUS AND HANUKKAH

The Enemy

In 168 BC, the Syrian emperor Antiochus came from the north and defeated Egypt. During the process of celebrating his victory, he was pressured by Rome to withdraw. In his anger at this reversal, he directed his resentment towards—and made a swath through—the land of the Jews. He set out to destroy Judaism, making any observance of the Jewish religion illegal. It is recorded that he would torture mothers and children publicly and then would execute them. He defiled the Temple by sacrificing a pig on the altar to the god Zeus Olympus and then looted the Temple (Daniel 8:11–19, 11:21–35).

The Hero

It looked as though this notorious Syrian emperor was unstoppable. However, in Modin, three miles north of Jerusalem, a Jew named Mattathias, along with his five sons, began a revolt against the Syrian monarch. This small band grew in number throughout the Judean hills and within three years drove the Syrian invaders out of Jerusalem and the surrounding area. It is said, that on the twenty-fifth day of Kislev (November/December), exactly three years to the day after its desecration, the Temple and altar were rededicated.

The Miracle

The Jews "wept" when they saw the desecration of the temple and began to restore it to a "state of ritual purity." Jewish tradition records that when the heroic Jews set about to rekindle the Perpetual Light (candle stand, seven-candle menorah), there was only enough consecrated oil to last only for one day. It would take eight days to prepare ritually permitted oil. The miracle was that the oil in the menorah, which was to last for only one day, remained lit for eight days until the special oil was procured.

The Rescue

Today, Jews throughout the world light candles each night during the eight-day celebration of this miracle of God. The miracle is the emphasis, not the military victory. Hanukkah, which means "dedication," proclaims a divine miracle, not a human victory. The reason the rabbis emphasize the spiritual, although the Bible regarded some wars as just, was simply that they did not allow human bloodshed to be associated with worship. David, for example, was not permitted to build the Temple because his life had been devoted to the quest of war. Hanukkah marks the rescue of Judaism, both as a faith and a way of life from annihilation.

The Twenty-Fifth Day

It is interesting how Hanukkah and Christmas are similar. Both originated in the same land by the same people, Israel and the Jews. Both are celebrated the same day in their respective months: the twenty-fifth day of Kislev (November/December) and the twenty-fifth day of December. Gifts are exchanged during these holidays, special foods are prepared, candles are lit, and spiritual songs are sung. Both commemorate a historical event.

The Servant

The servant is prominent in both holidays. The *shammash*, or servant candle, which is usually in the middle of the nine-candle menorah, or on the side of the menorah, is higher than the other eight candles. The *shammash* is used to light the other eight candles. The rabbis teach that it was the flame of faith which brought about the miracle. Its motto is found in the prophetic portion read during the festival: "Not by might, nor by power, but by my spirit, saith the Lord of Hosts" (Zechariah 4:6, KJV). The Hanukkah menorah is usually placed near a window so that all can see them from the street. This is in fulfillment of the rabbinic mandate "to publicize the miracle." According to Kabbalah (Jewish mysticism), the eight candles correspond to the name of God, which means "I shall be" (Exodus 3:14).

The Light

The *shammash* was given a special purpose: to light the other eight candles. On the first night, one candle is lit. The second night, two candles are lit. The third night, three candles are lit, and so on, until all eight candles are flickering with flame. The *shammash*, or the ninth candle, is the candle used to light the others. The flame of the *shammash* gives of itself to create an additional flame without losing any of its own brightness. Thus man gives of his love to his fellow man without losing anything of himself. The Messiah, who came not to be ministered to but to minister as a servant said, in the context of Hanukkah, "I am the light of the world; he that followeth me shall not walk in darkness, but shall have the light of life" (John 8:12, KJV). Just as the menorah is put in the window to pierce the darkness, so it is with Jesus, who pierces the darkness of the heart and brings light.

Also, Messiah Jesus said of himself in direct connection to Hanukkah, during the "feast of dedication" (Hanukkah), "I am the good shepherd (*shammash*), and the good shepherd (*shammash*) giveth his life for the sheep" (John 10:11, 22 KJV). Jesus chose Hanukkah as the time to reveal who he was. The evil Syrian Antiochus had a second name: Epiphanes. His complete name and title was King Antiochus Epiphanes. Epiphanes means "God manifest." You've guessed it: Antiochus called himself God. Jesus took this opportunity, during the celebration of Hanukkah, to proclaim that he is God (John 10:24–42). The psalmist said that there would be such a declaration: "I will declare the decree: the Lord hath said unto me, Thou art my Son; this day I have begotten thee" (Psalm 2:7). How do we know that the psalmist was speaking of Jesus? Luke confirms this when he wrote, "And we declare unto you glad tidings, how that the promise which was made unto the fathers, God hath fulfilled the same unto us their children, in that he hath raised up Jesus again; as it is also written in the second psalm, Thou art my Son, this day have I begotten thee" (Acts 13:32–33, KJV).

The Shema

Jesus said in John 10:30 during this time of Hanukkah, "I and My Father are one." This is another reminder of Antiochus. Jesus is saying that he was not only "God Manifest" but also "one" with God. The word translated "one" comes from the Hebrew *echad*, which is the same word used in Deuteronomy 6:4: "*Sh'ma, Yisra'el! Adonai Eloheinu, Adonai echad* [Hear, Israel! Adonai our God, Adonai is one]." Therefore, Jesus without a doubt said, "Israel, hear (listen to me Israel)! I am God."

The Resurrection

The apostle Paul described Jesus in connection with Hanukkah in Philippians 2:5-11. In these verses, you will find the Messiah lowering himself taking on the form of a servant, giving life to all who believe.

Jesus came not to be ministered to but to minister as a servant, shepherd, and light. The resurrection confirms who he said he was and is.

Beloved, may we be reminded of God's love for us—humbling himself, becoming a man, taking on the form of a servant, being born in Bethlehem's cave, born of virgin to die on a cross for our redemption and forgiveness. It is truly joyous to know that Jesus is the Light of the world! To believe in him is to receive the gift of eternal life.

"For God sent not his Son into the world to condemn the world; but that the world through him might be saved."

—JOHN 3:17 KJV

g. LIGHT

Light plays an important role in some religious traditions. For example, in the tradition of Judaism, lighting candles on Shabbat is to remind Jewish people of their Creator and to set apart this day from other days. Also, lighting the Hanukkah menorah is a memorial of the miracle of God's intervention on Israel's behalf in 168 B.C. Plus, the seven-branch menorah found in the synagogue and formerly in the Temple "tells of an eternal light of divine origin, but tended by man."[1] It is stated that this "holy lamp bore light in the Temple and from there to the world."[2] Even the "light" from Genesis 1:3, which was in existence before the luminaries (verses 14-19), "was a light, according to the [rabbinical] sages, set aside for the future of Messianic fulfillment."[3]

All these symbols point to God in one way or another. Unfortunately, many are blinded to the full meaning of the "Light." The Apostle Paul stated, "But even unto this day, when Moses is read, the veil is upon their heart" (2 Cor. 3:15, KJV).

"Light" in scripture is usually synonymous with God, hope, the "written" Word, or the "living" Word (Jesus). For example, we find in the Gospel of Luke, as the angelic announcement came to the shepherds concerning Christ's birth, that "the glory of the Lord shone round about them . . ." (Luke 2:9, KJV). The "glory" was this brilliant eternal light that terrified the shepherds as they realized they were in the presence of the Holy. Also, when Joseph and Mary entered the Temple with the baby Jesus in order to fulfill the custom of the Law (sacrifice for Mary's purification 40 days after the birth of a son), "a just and devout" man took the baby up in his arms and stated that Jesus is " light to lighten the Gentiles, and the glory of thy people Israel" (Luke 2:32, KJV).

Jesus said, "I am the light of the world: he that followeth me shall not walk in darkness, but shall have the light of life" (John 8:12, KJV).

"Darkness" describes the condition of a person's heart. One will stumble in the darkness unless they have a light to guide their way. Tradition, though beautiful, is not the "light." Religion, though commendable, is not the "light." Self-esteem and self-awareness, though important, are not the "light." The psalmist wrote, "Thy word is a lamp unto my feet, and a light unto my path" (Ps. 119:105, KJV). He found the secret to "dispel the darkness"—namely, the Word of God. The Apostle John stated, "In the beginning was the Word, and the Word was with God, and the Word was God . . . and the Word was made flesh, and dwelt among us" (John 1:1, 14, KJV).

Jesus, the Living Word, is the "Light" that dispels the darkness of sin from your heart. He is the "Passover Lamb," the one without spot or blemish, the perfect sacrifice on Calvary for the sins of the world. You see, without the shedding of blood there is no remission of sin (Heb. 9:22). This is why Jesus had to die on the cross and rise again.

Jesus Christ is "the true Light, which lighteth every man that cometh into the world" (John 1:9, KJV). The reason people do not come to the Light is because "there are insensitive hearts, still incapable of receiving this Light because the weight of their sins prevents them from seeing it. Let them not imagine that the Light is absent because they do not see it, for on account of their sins they are in darkness. 'And the light shineth in darkness; and the darkness comprehended it not' (John 1:5, KJV). Therefore . . . like the blind man exposed to the sun, the sun being present to him but he being absent from the sun, so the insensitive one, the sinner, the impious has a blind heart,"[4] wrote Augustine (354–430 AD).

Let us therefore examine our hearts to see if we are walking in the "Light" or walking in darkness. Do you know the Lord Jesus Christ as your personal Savior, or are you still walking in the darkness of darkness? Come to the Light and receive eternal life!

"Believe on the Lord Jesus Christ, and thou shalt be saved."

—Acts 16:31, KJV

Endnotes
1. Trepp, Leo. *A History of the Jewish Experience*. New York: Behrman House, Inc., 1973.
2. Blech, Benjamin. *More Secrets of Hebrew Words*. New Jersey: Jason Aronson, Inc., 1993.
3. Blech, Benjamin. *The Secrets of Hebrew Words*. New Jersey: Jason Aronson Inc., 1991.
4. Clark, Mary T. *Augustine of Hippo*. New Jersey: Paulist Press, New Jersey, 1984.

h. MOURNING LOST TEMPLES

Jews around the world are fast marking the beginning of an annual three-week mourning period commemorating the destruction of the first and second temples. The destruction of the Temples occurred on the ninth day of the month of Av (Tisha b'Av).

17th Day of Tammuz

However, the mourning starts three weeks before on the 17th day of the month of Tammuz, which is the day the Babylonian army marched into Jerusalem in 586 BC.

Other tragic events occurred on the 17th day of Tammuz: Moses broke the tablets in anger as the Israelites made the golden calf; blood sacrifices stopped at the first Temple one year before the Babylonians attacked; Noah sent a dove out of the ark on this day; the Romans breached the wall of Jerusalem in 70 AD.

Tisha b'Av

On this day not only were the First and Second Temple destroyed. Jewish tradition claims that after the Exodus, on this day, the Israelites were told they could not enter the Promised Land. During the Bar Kokhba Revolt, the last Jewish stronghold, called Bethar, fell on the Ninth of Av, 135 AD.

One year later, the Roman Emperor Hadrian set up a heathen temple on the site of the former Jewish Temple and rebuilt Jerusalem as a pagan city and refused to allow Jews to enter the Holy City. Also, on the Ninth of Av, 1492, the Christian rulers of Spain expelled from the land all the Jews who lived there for centuries.

How?

During these three weeks, some people abstain from certain foods and luxuries. The Book of Lamentations is read, oftentimes by candlelight, while sitting on the floor, with some sprinkle ashes on themselves. On Tisha b'Av, people in Jerusalem go to the Wall to mourn and pray.

The first word found in Lamentations is "how." Why was the city reduced to rubble by the invading Babylonian armies? Jeremiah, author of Lamentations, exposes his emotions. A death—a funeral—has occurred; Jerusalem lies barren.

What Can We Learn?

How could such a thing happen? Why tragedy?

1. God does punish disobedience. Amos 3:2 reminds us that even though God loves us and his covenant is eternal, he will punish disobedience. Approximately two million came out of Egypt with Moses; however, only two were allowed to enter the Land. The rest died in the wilderness for their disobedience.

2. Anyone, any church, any nation, any holy city, any sanctuary can disobey and find *Ichabod* or "the glory has departed" (1 Sam, 4:21; Jer. 7:12, 18:9, 25:8) written upon them by the hand of God himself. Those who are far from God will perish (Ps. 73:27).

3. There is hope. The Lord has/will comfort his people (Is. 52:9). God will make Jerusalem a delight and bless them in profound ways (Is. 60:15, 65:18, 19).

4. God restores and forgives. If a person, church, nation, or city confesses their sins and returns to God, he will forgive, restore, and heal (2 Chron. 7:14; 1 John 1:9).

Hebraic Thoughts

What Can We Do?

We must continue to pray for Israel during these last days. On one hand, Israel will experience more difficult days ahead; on the other hand, we are promised that Israel will experience, in this day of grace, a "remnant" that will believe (Rom. 11:5).

i. PERSEVERANCE THROUGH HARD TIMES

2 Chronicles 20

Judah, the southern kingdom (Israel is now divided) was like a superpower in the days of old. They were enjoying victory and peace and other nations feared their strength. Jehoshaphat, king of Judah, was a godly king who loved the Lord, and through him God would bring renewal and spiritual awakening to Judah. He made alliances with others and fortified and supplied defense emplacements in Judah. He enrolled an army of 780,000 men of Judah and 380,000 men of Benjamin. This did not include those stationed in the fortifications. Jehoshaphat, had just returned in peace and safety from his involvement with Ahab, king of Israel, against the Syrians.

Deception

Ahab, king of the Northern Kingdom Israel, wanted to have Jehoshaphat join him in battle against Syria. (You may recall that Ahab's infamous wife was Jezebel). Jehoshaphat's son married Ahab and Jezebel's daughter. Jehoshaphat agreed to go to war alongside Ahab against the Syrians on one condition: that the Lord would give his approval. Ahab, being a wicked king as he was, attempted to deceive Jehoshaphat through some 400 false prophets who would say that God would allow them to be victorious in battle.

Didn't Listen

However, Jehoshaphat sent for a true prophet and the prophet said that they were going to lose the battle. Ahab mistreated the prophet and put him in prison. Unfortunately, Jehoshaphat didn't listen to the prophet, and he and Ahab went into battle. Ahab lost his life and Jehoshaphat made it safely back to Jerusalem.

Doing the Right Thing

But as he came back, he was met by another prophet. As a result of this encounter and recent defeat, the king began to make reforms within Judah. Just when Judah was getting back on track as a nation, war was declared. Three armies came together from the other side of the Dead Sea and were now in En Gedi, just 20 miles from Jerusalem. In spite of Judah being a superpower, Jehoshaphat feared because of the prophet's warning of God's wrath. So the King declared a national day of prayer and fasting. God answered their prayers.

When difficult times come, what do we do? What have we learned from this lesson?

1. Don't be afraid; trust in the Lord (20:15–17).
2. Worship and bow down before the Lord (20:18).
3. Praise the Lord with passion (20:19).
4. Have faith in the Lord (20:20).
5. Sing, praise, and give thanks (20:21).
6. Rejoice in the Lord Almighty (20:27).
7. Celebrate the Lord (20:28).

When the choices are hard, when we're battered and scarred, when we've spent our resources, when we've given our all in Jesus' name, we press on. We stay the course! Songwriter Rich Mullins penned: "So if I stand, let me stand on the promise that you will pull me through. And if I can't, let me fall on the grace that first brought me to you. And if I sing, let me sing for the joy that has born in me these songs. And if I weep, let it be as a man who is longing for his home."

Stay the course! If we do these things, there will be peace and rest that comes from the Lord (verse 30; Isaiah 40).

j. MYSTERIES: TISHA B' AV

Tisha B' Av, on the ninth of the month of Av, commemorates the destruction of the First and Second Temples in Jerusalem.

On the evening of the holiday, the lights are dimmed in the synagogue and the congregants sit on low benches or on the floor. Readings will be from the Book of Lamentations along with other portions of scripture that focuses on mourning and prayer. That evening, a fast begins.

The ninth of Av is has a significant history for the Jews. In 135 AD, the Bar *Kochba* (a false messiah) revolt against the Romans ended in defeat on the ninth of Av. One year later, on the ninth of Av, the Roman emperor Hadrian had the ruins of Jerusalem plowed under by teams of oxen and built a Roman city on its site, calling it Aelia Capitolina, and Jews were forbidden to enter the city upon penalty of death. In 1242, Talmudic books were burned in Paris on the ninth of Av. In 1492, Jews were driven out of Spain on the ninth of Av. In 1942, Jews were deported from the Warsaw Ghetto to the Treblinka death camp on the ninth of Av.

"This is why I weep and my eyes overflow with tears" (Lamentations 1:16, NIV).

We don't always have the answer for life's questions. God's ways and thoughts are bigger than our understanding (Isa. 55:8, 9). There are many mysteries that only God knows why they happen. One mystery is Tisha B' Av.

k. OUR DEBT: PART ONE

To say Christians owe a debt to the Jew is an understatement. The foundation upon which New Testament faith rests is the Hebrew Bible. The *Tenach*, or the Hebrew Bible (Old Testament), is comprised of three major divisions: Torah (the five books of Moses), *Nevi'im* (the Prophets), and *Ketuvim* (the Writings).

All that Christians hold dear is derived from Judaism in some form. From the pews, altar, pulpit, baptism, officers of the church, and our reverence of the Scriptures stems from first-century Judaism.

Jesus was Jewish. The Bible is a Jewish book written by Jewish writers (with one or two exceptions) about a Jewish Messiah who will bring redemption and a kingdom of universal peace. The Jewish apostles took the gospel to the Gentiles. Subsequently, all Gentiles who attend church on Sunday can thank the Jews for bringing them the message of Jesus the Messiah.

Believers owe a debt of gratitude and thanksgiving to the Jew. We can do this in part by learning about the Jewish culture, religion, and how to communicate the gospel message effectively and lovingly.

Both Jewish and Gentile People Need Jesus

Romans 1:16 (KJV) states, "For I am not ashamed of the gospel of Christ: for it is the power of God unto salvation to everyone that believeth; to the Jew first, and also to the Greek." Wherever Paul traveled, he would address the Jews in that community first, then the Gentiles.

1. Jewish people need Messiah. All people, regardless of nationality or ethnic origin, are under sin (Romans 3:9). There is not a separate method of salvation for the Jew. All people, both Jew and Gentile, are guilty before God and are in need of redemption (Romans 3:19).

2. Jesus commands us to share the gospel with all people (Mark 16:15). Some Christians, even within the evangelical community, hold to a presupposition that the Jewish community has no need of hearing the gospel. However, Jesus commands us to go and communicate to both Jew and Gentile.

3. The Apostle Paul reveals his burden for the Jewish people in Romans chapters nine, ten, and eleven. He expresses that having a concern for Israel's salvation is part of God's plan for the human race. He emphasized that God has not cast away his people. God loves them with an everlasting love. Paul also enforced the reality that the Gentiles owe a great debt to the Jews. The non-Jew has been the recipient of the Word of God, the hope of Israel, through the Messiah and eternal life with God because of the faithfulness of Jewish people taking the gospel to them. The great apostle stresses that there will be a day when Israel will become God's witness to the world, therefore having a special place in God's program.

l. OUR DEBT: PART TWO

"And I will make of thee a great nation, and I will bless thee, and make thy name great; and thou shalt be a blessing: And I will bless them that bless thee."

—Genesis 12:2, 3, KJV

The blessing is sixfold:

1. *I will make of thee a great nation.* Through Abraham came the Jewish nation. Also through Abraham came a spiritual heritage to those of like faith. Plus, through Ishmael came the Arab nations.

2. *I will bless thee.* This was evident through the earthly blessings he received along the way. Plus, he was considered a friend of God (James 2:23).

3. *And make thy name great.* Abraham's name is respected within the Jewish, Moslem, and Christian communities. Along with the name of Christ, Abraham is one of the most widely known throughout the world.

4. *And thou shalt be a blessing.* This expands throughout the world of both Jews and Gentiles. Abraham is an example of a man of great faith in God.

5. *And I will bless them that bless thee, and curse him that curseth thee.* History verifies this statement. Those individuals and nations who helped Israel were blessed and those who stood against Israel were indeed cursed.

6. *And in thee shall all the families of the earth be blessed.* This promise projects the coming of the Messiah from the seed of Abraham and considers all that Messiah is and will be. Below is a list of some of the messianic prophecies fulfilled in Jesus of Nazareth.

Messianic Prophecies

Prophecy	OT Location	NT Fulfillment
Seed of a woman	Gen. 3:15	1 Jn. 3:18; Gal. 4:4
Seed of Abraham	Gen. 12:3	Matt. 1:1
Tribe of Judah	Gen. 49:10	Heb.7:14; Matt. 1
Seed of David	Ps. 89:4; 132:11	Lk.1:22; Acts 2:29
Born in Bethlehem	Micah 5:2	Matt. 2; Luke 2
Virgin Birth	Isa. 7:14	Matt. 1; Luke 1
Like Moses	Deut. 18:15, 18	John 7; Acts 3
Triumphal Entry	Zech. 9:9	Matt. 21; John 12
Rejected	Isa. 53; Psa. 118	Jn. 1; Matt. 26
Betrayed	Psa. 41:9	Matt. 26; Mark 14

Prophecy	OT Location	NT Fulfillment
30 Pieces of Silver	Zech 11:12	Matt. 26
Forsaken	Zech. 13:7	Matt. 26
Condemned	Isa. 53:8	Matt. 27; Lk. 23
Silent	Isa. 53:7	Matt. 27; Lk. 23
Smitten, Spat Upon	Isa. 50:6; Mic. 5:1	Matt. 26; Lk. 22
Mocked	Psa. 22:7, 8	Matt. 28:38–43
Crucifixion	Psa. 22:14, 16, 17	Matt. 27; Jn. 19
Suffer with Transgressors	Isa. 53:12	Matt. 27; Lk. 23
Casting of Lots	Psa. 22:18	Matt. 27; Mk. 15
No Broken Bones	Exod. 12:46	John 19:31–36
Sacrificial Death	Isa. 53: 5–12	John 1:11; Acts 10
Rise Again	Psa. 16:10	Acts 2; Mark 16
At God's Right Hand	Psa. 110:1	Mark 16; Luke 24

m. REPENTANCE—*TESHUVAH*

"Repent, and turn from all your transgressions, so that iniquity will not be your ruin."

—EZEKIEL 18:30

When was the last time you heard a sermon on sin and repentance? Blaming others for our problems is a propensity that has become popular in some Christian circles. "Sin" and "repentance" seemingly have been erased from our vocabulary and thinking process. Whatever happened to accountability? I'm speaking of accountability to ourselves and especially to God.

Teshuvah is the Hebrew term for repentance. Jewish tradition teaches that repentance is motivated by two factors: fear and love—fear of the punishment from God and love for God. The Scripture is infused with the teaching of repentance and yet very little is said about this important doctrine. Jesus said, "Unless you repent you will all likewise perish" (Luke 13:3, 5).

In Luke's Gospel, we find an account of a woman, a "sinner," who heard that Jesus was nearby. We read, "And behold, a woman in the city who was a sinner, when she knew that Jesus sat at the table in the

Pharisee's house, brought an alabaster flask of fragrant oil, and stood at his feet behind him weeping; and she began to wash, his feet with her tears, and wiped them with the hair of her head; and she kissed his feet and anointed them with the fragrant oil" (Luke 7:37–38).

Please notice that she did not look into the face of our Lord. The awareness of her sin and his holiness was real, which motivated her sense of humility. Trembling and weeping, wiping her tears with the hairs of her head, she now begins to kiss his feet again and again, anointing them with perfume. True repentance brings about genuine affection for God.

Jesus responded to her passion and sincerity as she turned from her sin by stating, "Your sins are forgiven . . . Your faith has saved you. Go in peace" (verses 48 and 50).

Repentance is turning from sin, changing one's mind, understanding the necessity of knowing God. Just as this dear woman had an acute awareness of her sin and a need for the Savior, we too must experience repentance that brings about the "New Birth" (John 3:3, 7).

The Lord through the prophet Ezekiel (18:30–32) reminds us that we must "[r]epent, and turn" and "ast away" our transgressions. Notice the phrases "your transgressions," "your ruin," and "turn and live." This is why Jesus was "wounded for our transgressions, [and] he was bruised for our iniquities: the chastisement of our peace was upon him; and with his stripes we are healed" (Isaiah 53:5).

Let us not lose sight of the reality of sin and the need for repentance in this age of psychobabble. With the woman in Luke 7 in mind, let us take to heart the truth of our Lord's words: "Come to me all you who labor and are heavy laden, and I will give you rest. Take my yoke upon you and learn from me, for I am gentle and lowly in heart and you will find rest for your souls. For my yoke is easy and my burden is light" (Matthew 11:28–30).

n. SEASONS TO REMEMBER

What an interesting time in history! Each year is full of Jewish and Christian holidays.

Judaism's Holy Days cover the celebration of a New Year (Rosh Hashanah); the solemn days of prayers, repentance, and self-examination leading up to Yom Kippur; the conclusion of the annual reading of Torah (*Simchat Torah*), parading the Scroll in celebration; Hanukkah, remembering victory and a miracle lighting candles in remembrance;

and Purim, reading the story of Esther and in costume reenacting God's protection of the Jewish people.

Christianity's Holy Days include four weeks of preparation time for the celebration of the Nativity of Jesus called Advent; Christmas, remembering the Incarnation (God becoming man); Epiphany, which celebrates the birth of Jesus, the visit from the scholars acknowledging the important role this child will have on the human race; and Lent, which is a time of prayer, fasting, and self-examination, thus imitating Jesus' wilderness experience.

The similarities are amazing—repentance, fasting, prayers, celebration of miracles, lighting candles, remembering the stories of Scripture and the survival of God's chosen people, and God communicating and revealing redemption to the human race through his Anointed One.

Engage

These Holy Days cause an effect on people. Biblical Christianity and Judaism teach us to have faith and encourage us to engage our world. We are called to respond to God, who reveals himself to us in the person of Christ Jesus (Messiah Yeshua). It is a call to action before God and man.

The Middle East is unraveling before our eyes. Nations are calling for the division of Israel or its destruction. Armies are jockeying for position and politicians are exercising their art of prattle.

Our hope does not rest with politicians or with soldiers or with religious radicals; our hope rests secure with Christ Jesus our Lord.

Action

As believers we are called to action before God and man. Therefore, we must:

1. Pray for the peace of Jerusalem (Psalm 122:6; Mat. 6:10; Rev. 22:20)
2. Love God with a passion (Deut. 6:5; Mat. 22:37)
3. Love your neighbor (Mat. 22:39)
4. Bless Abraham's seed (Gen. 12:1–3)
5. Bless the children (Mat. 19:14; 25:40)

Time is short, life is precious, and Jesus is coming soon!

o. SHAVUOT: FEAST OF PENTECOST

Shavuot, or the Feast of Pentecost, is one of the seven feasts described in Leviticus 23. Originally, Shavuot was an agricultural feast. Eventually, it became known as the day Moses received the Law from Mt. Sinai.

Historically, the Jews would celebrate by reading the Book of Exodus, focusing on the account of Moses receiving the Law. Also, the Book of Ruth would be read because of her devotion to the Law of God. Today, this tradition is still in vogue. Plus, thousands in Jerusalem, after studying the Scriptures all night, will trek to the Western Wall and as the sun rises recite a morning liturgical prayer.

Shavuot is celebrated in late May or early June 50 days after Passover. Historically, during the Passover, after the sacrificing of the lamb, 600,000 men (Exodus 12:37–38)—approximately 3,000,000 Israelites total—left Egypt after being slaves for 400 years. Now they are free!

What an awesome sight afterwards for the Israelites to behold God's power at the Red Sea, then to receive manna from Heaven and water from the rock. Now, standing at the foot of a quaking Mt. Sinai in the desert, they observe Moses, their leader and deliverer, ascend up into the very presence of God. It had been almost 2,000 years since God displayed such communication to a man. Now, Moses is prostrate in his presence and the Jews are terrified.

Moses was gone for 40 days on the quaking mountain. The people became impatient and disobedient to God, making and erecting a Golden Calf. The Israelites began to worship this image of gold, and as a punishment for their sin, 3,000 died by the sword of the Levites (Exodus 32:28).

Fifteen hundred years after the Exodus, following the sacrifice of Jesus (Yeshua), our "Passover Lamb" on Calvary, the Church was born. During Shavuot (Pentecost), the disciples, being in the upper room, were filled with the Holy Spirit. Peter began to preach, which resulted in 3,000 souls being saved (Acts 2:41).

Look at the contrast! When the Law was given, 3,000 died. When the birthday of the Church unfolded, 3,000 received life! Paul stated, "The law was our schoolmaster to bring us unto Christ (Messiah)" (Galatians 3:24). The Law, therefore, being holy (Romans 7:12), points us to someone greater than itself, namely Messiah. The Law is holy and we would not have known about sin except through the Law (Romans 7:7,

12). "But where sin abounded, grace did much more abound" (Romans 5:20).

Grace reigns in Jesus our Messiah. Life, peace, and purpose are found in him. Therefore, Shavuot, or the Feast of Pentecost, directs us to a truth greater than the Law. It is through the Lord Jesus and his shed blood that anyone who trusts in him will be set free from the condemnation of the Law. Eternal life is the gift for those who believe. This is the message Peter preached on Shavuot as he proclaimed Jesus to be both "Lord and Messiah" by virtue of the resurrection (Acts 2:14–36).

> *"For the law was given by Moses, but grace and truth came by Jesus Christ."*
>
> —John 1:17, KJV

This is the message of the Church that was birthed on the day of Shavuot. The Church is the mystery that was originally hidden, but now revealed (Ephesians 3). The Church is the representation of the Lord Jesus on earth. Therefore, let the Church manifest grace and truth. May the Church reflect Jesus!

p. IT BEGAN WITH A SIGH!

When people begin to cry out and recognize their hopelessness without God without divine intervention, only then will they move toward and with God.

After centuries of bondage, slavery, defeat, and disconnect, God's ancient people lost their strength, courage, and faith. Their dreams were shattered and tossed to the wind. When it seemed they came to the end of the road, we read:

> *"And it came to pass in process of time, that the king of Egypt died; and the children of Israel sighed by reason of the bondage, and they cried, and their cry came up unto God by reason of the bondage. And God heard their groaning, and God remembered his covenant with Abraham, with Isaac, and with Jacob. And God looked upon the Children of Israel, and God had respect unto them."*
>
> —Exodus 2:23–25, KJV

When a people lose hope in the sight of God, and when a people stop dreaming and trusting in God, selfishness unfolds. Corruption increases, looking to other gods for security begins, and a sense of ricocheting through life without direction intensifies.

Only when Israel sighed, when they paused and looked inside their heart and truly saw their need, and cried unto God, God heard and deliverance and redemption was provided through the blood of the Lamb. On that day thousands of years ago, Israel was delivered from physical and spiritual bondage.

Four Questions

Four questions are asked today during the Passover tradition; usually the youngest child at the *seder* (meal) asks these questions. However, anyone may recite these questions, not just children.

(Introduction)—Why is this night different from all other nights?

1. Why is it that on all other nights we eat either bread or *matzah*, but on this night we only eat *matzah*?
2. Why is it that on all other nights we eat all vegetables, but on this night we eat only bitter herbs?
3. Why is it that on all other nights we do not dip even once, but on this night we dip twice?
4. Why is it that on all other nights we eat when we are sitting or reclining, but on this night we eat while reclining?

With almost a million children hungry in Israel, perhaps the questions children will ask will be these (as suggested by a Jerusalem Post ad):

(Introduction)—Why is this night same as all other nights?
1. Why are my shoes to small for my feet?
2. Why is there no food in the house?
3. Mommy, why do you cry all the time?
4. Why aren't we having a *seder* (meal) like all my friends?

Israel still needs redemption and deliverance, both physically as well as spiritually. Israel Today Ministries has touched thousands with the love of Jesus providing thousands of meals and communicating the gospel.

q. THE SEVENTH MONTH: PART ONE
Leviticus 23:23–44

Festive lights. Special foods. Games. Family celebration. Prayer. Religious activity. Strange-looking tents. What is going on within the Jewish community? Why are Jewish people praying, fasting, and rejoicing?

The number seven has always been a special biblical number according to scholars. This sacred number speaks of completion, perfection, and points to God's divine purpose.

During the seventh month of the Jewish calendar (September 12, 2007, beginning at sundown), you will find the Jewish community worldwide getting ready for the most important events of the Jewish calendar: the High Holy Days of Rosh HaShanah and Yom Kippur (the Day of Atonement). In addition, another holy day, Sukkot (Feast of Tabernacles), is also in the seventh month (Tishri).

Let's take a brief look at these very important holy days, moments of festivity, reflection, awe, and self-examination.

Rosh HaShanah

Rosh HaShanah (the first day of Tishri) is the beginning of the Hebrew year. "Rosh" means "head" or "beginning" or the "start of" the new year. This is a time when Jews celebrate the anniversary of the creation of the world, universe, and man (Genesis 1, 2). Rosh HaShanah is a time of rejoicing and celebration as well as time of deep reflection and holy occasion (Leviticus 23:24; Numbers 29:1–6; Nehemiah 8:2, 9–12).

God Judges

Rosh HaShanah, according to Jewish tradition, is when God looks into the hearts of people and judge their deeds and motives. It is said that God will inscribe their names in the Books of Life or Death, and in so doing will determine who will live another year or who will die. Subsequently, Rosh HaShanah is not only a time to celebrate the Jewish new year and the creation, but it also begins what is called the "Ten Days of Awe or Penitence." Multitudinous prayers are offered, and scripture reading and repentance culminates on Yom Kippur ten days after Rosh HaShanah begins. The prayers, good deeds, and repentance are done while the people are hopeful that God will look with favor upon their lives and inscribe their name in the Book of Life. To symbolize purity, some of the men will wear a white robe to the synagogue. These will be the shrouds in which the observant Jews are buried.

The Sounding of the Trumpet

Rosh HaShanah is also known as the Feast of Trumpets or Yom *Teruah* (the Day of the Sounding of the Shofar), *Yom ha-Din* (the Day of Judgment), and *Yom ha-Zikkaron* (the Day of Remembrance). During this holiday the *shofar*, or ram's horn, is blown. To be in Israel during this time is quite an experience. You will hear trumpet after trumpet piercing the crisp autumn air. The rabbis open the Ark of the Torah, and the story of Abraham and the binding of Isaac is remembered.

In remembering the story of Abraham and Isaac, the religious are reminded of Isaac's rescue from death and the demonstration of God's mercy. The night before the holiday, Jews greet one another with "*L'Shanah tovah tikatevu*"—"May you be inscribed for a good year!" Apples or bread are dipped in honey to express hope and sweetness for a good next year, and prayers for the peace of the world are spoken as they remember God.

Throwing Stones

Regarding the idea of repentance and new life, you will find the religious going to streams or rivers, observing the water current moving down, symbolically or in reality, to the sea. Some of the faithful are able to go directly to the ocean, depending on where they live. They recite the last verses from the book of the prophet Micah which states, "And thou will cast their sins into the depths of the sea" (Micah 7:19, KJV).

Beforehand, they will fill their pockets with stones, herbs, or flowers, which symbolically represent their sins. Standing at the shore, the religious will cast the symbol of their sins into the water. The idea is that the current then takes their sin into the depths of the sea, never to be seen again. How comforting that thought is to the contrite soul! This is done on the first afternoon of the first day of Rosh HaShanah and is called *Tashlikh*, or Casting Off. Therefore, by exercising this act, they symbolically cast their sins into the water.

So, in the final analysis, Rosh HaShanah is a celebration of the anniversary of God creating the universe. God is remembered as the Supreme Judge and Sovereign over all things known and unknown and as the Living and Everlasting God. It is a time to remember that God holds our very breath in his hands and that we must give an account for our sins and trust in God's forgiveness and mercy.

Rosh HaShanah reminds us of new beginnings and accountability. It draws our attention to the creation of new life and meditation upon the One who created all life. Jesus said, "I am the way, the truth, and the life: no man cometh unto the Father, but by me" (John 14:6, KJV). John the Apostle tells us that Jesus is the source of all life and that it will be the Son of God who passes judgment, not the Father (John 1, 5:22). Also, it was Jesus who created all things and that "he is before all things, and by him all things consist" (John 1; Colossians 1:16, 17, KJV). Plus, as mentioned earlier, the Apostle Paul, referencing the tradition of Rosh HaShanah, stated that when the trumpet (*shofar*, or ram's horn) of God is blown, the dead in Christ shall rise first (1 Thessalonians 4:16). Paul brings a clearer focus on this in 1 Corinthians 15:52 (KJV) when he says, "In a moment, in the twinkling of an eye, at the last trump: for the trumpet shall sound, and the dead shall be raised incorruptible." In Jewish tradition, the blowing of the *shofar* is said to confound Satan. The trumpet sounds the coming of Messiah and the Kingdom of God. Satan despises and resists this moment.

Isn't it truly amazing that the celebration of Rosh HaShanah was actually a foreshadow, a presage, a rehearsal for the celebration of the Messiah? This being the case, all people must examine the claims of Jesus. Is he the Messiah, as he said (Matthew 27:63, 64; Mark 14:61, 62; John 4:25, 26)? If he is the Messiah, the Creator of life, and the Judge, then we must respond, either in belief or rejection. If we reject Jesus as the Messiah and Lord, we of all people will be most miserable and the eternal ramifications are very ominous (John 3:36). If we believe, then we will find peace, purpose, and meaning to our lives, and the eternal ramifications are very encouraging (John 3:16).

r. THE SEVENTH MONTH: PART TWO

Leviticus 23:23–44

Yom Kippur

Yom Kippur (10th of Tishri)—or, literally, Day of Atonement—is the last of the Ten Days of Awe or Penitence and is the holiest day in the Jewish calendar (Leviticus 23:27–32). It is known as "the Sabbath of Sabbaths." It is marked by twenty-four hours of prayer and fasting.

White is the symbol of purity and is the dominant color of Yom Kippur. The altar cloths and the Torah covers, which are maroon on the Sabbaths and blue on the festivals, are now changed to white. The story of Jonah is recited, as he was the prophet who learned that all men are God's children (according to Jewish tradition). The very pious recite responsively the entire Book of Psalms.

The Yom Kippur service is the longest in the Jewish liturgy. It begins with the chanting of the *Kol Nidre*, a prayer asking for the release from vows and promises that were not kept. Prayers continue throughout the evening and the next day. Confession of sins, or the *Viddui*, is expressed. The service closes with the *Neilah*, or closing. It refers to the closing of the gates of Heaven at the conclusion of the day. Finally, the *shofar* is blown and these words are exclaimed: "*Leshanah habaah biyerushalayim!*" ("Next year in Jerusalem!") At the close of this very somber holy day, there is a sense of relief that God's wrath is postponed. Immediately, families begin to build *sukkahs* (tabernacles).

Regarding Yom Kippur, the holiest day in Judaism, we must tie together the two holidays. Rosh HaShanah is the beginning of something that will culminate at Yom Kippur.

From the first day, throwing the stones in the water (*Tashlikh*) until final blowing of the *shofar* at the conclusion of Yom Kippur, the emphasis is on repentance and trying to appease the judgment of God.

Remember, it was on the Day of Atonement the high priest went into the Holy of Holies to offer sacrifice on behalf of Israel. Therefore, we can understand the effort of modern day Judaism in trying to create a sobriety and reverence for such an important day.

Wait a minute! The Temple is gone. The Holy of Holies is gone.

Since the Temple no longer exists, it is impossible to offer blood atonement for the people. So, what the rabbis have done is substitute blood atonement with mitzvah, a ritual obligation(s) or good deed(s).

Now we have a problem. The Scripture teaches "for it is the blood that maketh an atonement for the soul" (Leviticus 17:11). Good deeds are commendable; however, they cannot atone for the soul. Religious ritual obligation is commendable; however, rituals cannot atone for the soul.

The Scripture also teaches that without the shed blood there is no remission of sin (Hebrews 9:22). What is the answer to this problem?

Yeshua (Yeshua is the Hebrew way to say Jesus) is the answer. He was the perfect and final sacrifice for sin (Hebrews 6–9).

Therefore, Yom Kippur and Rosh HaShanah direct us to the One who can forgive sin and bring into a right relationship with God. Jesus is God's Lamb, offered for the sins of mankind. We must put our trust in him and not depend on our own religious efforts or good deeds to gain God's approval, for eternal life is a gift received through faith and is not predicated on good deeds or religious activity (Ephesians 2:8–10). We must trust in God's mercy and grace provided for us through his Messiah, the Lord Jesus, the Lamb of God who takes away the sin of the world (John 1:29; Psalm 49:7–9; Isaiah 59:12; Leviticus 9:12; Jeremiah 31:3; Leviticus 17:11; Isaiah 53:3–10; Psalm 2:12; Proverbs 30:4; Genesis 15:6; John 11:25–26; John 14:6).

s. THE SEVENTH MONTH: PART THREE

Leviticus 23:23–44

Sukkot

Sukkot, or the Feast of Tabernacles, begins on the fifteenth day of the seventh month (Leviticus 23:39). Sukkot is a harvest festival of thanksgiving. It is a time of remembering the wandering Israelites in the wilderness for forty years living in temporary dwellings or booths (a *sukkah*).

Sukkot (Tabernacles) is the completion of both Passover and Pentecost. During Passover, the "wave sheaf," or the first ripe grain, was offered as a sign of more harvest to come. At Pentecost, more harvest was completed, as the wheat and barley became ripe. These wave loaves were presented to the Lord as a precursor to more harvest yet to come. During Sukkot, the whole harvest came into being (grapes, apples, nuts, pomegranates, etc.). Sukkot points us to the Millennial Reign of Messiah on earth (Revelation 21:3; Zechariah 14; Ezekiel 40–48).

God intends to illustrate during this seven-day feast during the seventh month a picture for us of the final harvest and redemptive work on earth. It is a time in which the fruit of our lives will finally be ready to be gathered in the God's storehouses. This is the day for which God has waited and foretold, "Therefore be patient, brethren, until the coming of the Lord. See how the farmer waits for the precious fruit of the earth, waiting patiently for it until it receives the early and latter rain" (James 5:7).

t. TIMES OF THE GENTILES

Jerusalem is the most loved and desired city in history. Those who control Jerusalem control the destiny of humanity.

Jesus said that "Jerusalem shall be trodden down of the Gentiles, until the times of the Gentiles be fulfilled" (Lk. 21:24, KJV). The times of the Gentiles began in 605 BC, when Nebuchadnezzar conquered Jerusalem taking captives to Babylon. Down through history, we see Israel in Jerusalem, but not necessarily in control of Jerusalem. At the time of Jesus, Israel was present in Jerusalem; however, the Romans were in control. Even today, some would argue that Israel is in Jerusalem, but not in total control. (The Temple Mount area is currently controlled by Muslims and not directly under Jewish rule).

We understand that "the times of the Gentiles" is likely referring to Daniel's prophecy in chapters 2 and 7, which teaches that the Gentiles will rule the planet until the coming of the Messiah. When Messiah returns, he will establish the Millennial Kingdom where he will rule and reign from Jerusalem for a thousand years. Then Israel will be completely restored and redeemed (Isa. 49).

In the twentieth century, the world observed the beginning of Israel's restoration, and in 1948, a state was born. Nineteen years later, a Soviet-led coalition of Arab states attempted to crush the tiny nation. In six days, Israel miraculously defeated the enemy and took Jerusalem in this manner for the first time in 2,500 years.

God promised that Israel would be restored in the last days—in fact, Ezekiel 36 – 40 teaches that the restoration will be progressive, culminating in the Millennial Kingdom.

In these tumultuous days, may we who believe in the Lord Jesus and the teaching of Scripture "[p]ray for the peace of Jerusalem: for they shall prosper that love thee" (Psalm 122:6, KJV)!

u. TREASURES IN THE SAND

Moses gave his final blessing on the twelve tribes of Israel and saying to Zebulun, "For they shall partake of the abundance of the seas and of treasures hidden in the sand" (Deut. 33:19).

For years, the Tribe of Zebulun would argue, "Where are the treasures in the sand?" Sometime later it was discovered that you could turn sand into glass. It is said that the ancient Greeks declared that the secret of glassmaking started on coastline of Haifa.

Blue String

The Scripture speaks of the proper way to make *tzitzis*, or the four corners of the prayer shawl, which are very important in Judaism and Messianic communities (Num. 15:38–40; Deut. 22:12). The command contained a mandate regarding a blue string. The blue dye used to make this string came from the blood of a snail, called *Chilazon*, found only near Haifa, or the Tribe of Zebulun. The blue dye from this little snail was used to fulfill God's command; thus, Zebulun partook of the abundance of the seas in this regard.

Triangle Mountain

Rising up from Haifa is a triangular-shaped mountain called Mount Carmel. A wooded range covers approximately 13 miles of this distinctive peninsula, which drops sharply into the Mediterranean. This is such a beautiful area that Scripture often refers to it as a symbol of majesty and blessing (2 Chron. 26:10; SOS 7:5; Isa. 35:2; Jer. 46:18, 50:19). When Carmel suffered, it was an indication of God's judgment (Nah. 1:4; Amos 1:2; Isa. 33:9).

Scorching the Earth

This was an area in which many Canaanite shrines and altars were located and caves where hermits lived (Amos 9:3). An ancient altar to the God of Israel also stood on the mountain (1 Kings 18:19–39). The prophet Elijah chose to do battle with the prophets of Ba'al on this location. The story declares that the God of Israel proved he was the true God by consuming Elijah's offering with fire so hot that it melted the stones of the altar and scorched the earth surrounding the area.

Raindrops Keep Falling on My Head

During a great drought in Israel, the Prophet went to the top of Carmel and prayed for rain. A tiny cloud about the size of a man's fist appeared over the Mediterranean. The cloud grew and eventually the sky was filled with dark, thundering rain clouds, and the drought ended (1 Kings 18:42–45).

Legends

1. Snakes

One legend states that Hiel, the one who attempted to rebuild Jericho at the cost of the life of his sons (fulfilling Joshua's prophecy, Jos. 6:26; 1 Kings 16:34), was hiding in the wood of the altar to Ba'al, and if Ba'al would not answer he would secretly light the fire. However, the legend continues, a poisonous snake slithered into the pile of wood and bit him and he died, unable to deceive the people of Israel.

2. Rocks

Another legend concerning Mount Carmel is that Elijah was hungry and asked a farmer for one of his melons. The farmer replied that these were not melon but rocks. The so-called miracle was when all the melons turned into rocks. Today, on the mountain, they say that you can pick up these small rocks and tap them and they will sound like you are tapping a melon.

3. Flowers

A flower you find readily on Mount Carmel is the cyclamen. The flower looks like a small crown. Most flowers open up and reach for the sky, but not so with the cyclamen. It humbly bows its head toward the ground as though it is in mourning. For years, people have said that this humble flower is waiting for the coming of the Messiah, when the crown of glory will be restored to Israel—then it will gladly lift its crowned head toward the sky. You get the idea; the mountain is a very special place.

Comforting Cave

At the foot of Carmel is a cave that overlooks the emerald blue-green Mediterranean. The sea breeze caresses the trees and wildflowers along the mountainside. This part of the world would remind you of San Diego, California. The cave is where Elijah stayed for refuge from Ahab, for rest, and for prayer; it was his home. It is revered by Jews, Christians, and Muslims.

Today, you can walk on a pathway up to the cave, which has been turned into a place of worship and prayer. On the walls you will find etched ancient inscriptions in Greek, along with Jewish and Christian symbols. A wooden wall divides the men from the women. Scripture pages in frames telling the story of Elijah hang on the wall. There is a special place for private prayers behind a heavy, ornate curtain that hangs high above.

Men and women praying and reading cry out to God. People there worship and adore God, hoping that a miracle will take place regarding their prayers. Why? Simply because the holy prophet lived here and miracles happened through him.

Those worshipping, praying, and seeking God's approval are generally Jewish. You may find a few Gentile tourists (obviously believers) visiting with great reverence. Perhaps you may find Moslems praying there, but not usually.

Confluence

Israel is a confluence of monotheistic faith, where there is harmony combined with terror. There are no simple answers, as many would like to believe. Politicians cannot bring lasting peace, soldiers cannot create permanent security, and religionists cannot enlighten the souls of individuals.

It is only through Messiah Jesus that lasting peace will occur and ultimate security will abound. And only the Anointed One foretold of old, the One who died and rose again the third day, can truly enlighten the souls of individuals for those who believe (John 1:9, 14:6).

Evil Leaders

A couple of years ago, rockets fell here in the north, destroying and killing with the purpose of annihilating the Jews. Yes, in this incredible place of biblical history, miracles, and hope, evil men bent on wiping Israel off the map attacked. Clouds still loom and nefarious leaders still beat the drums of war. Pray for peace, pray for Jerusalem, and pray for God's ancient people. The time to stand in the gap is now. Like the Prophet Elijah, stand, even when no one else stands with you. Stand alone if you have to. Nevertheless, stand.

5

List Lessons

a. GOD IS MANY THINGS

In Genesis: He is the Creator and Seed of the woman (1:1; 3:15)

In Exodus: He is the Lamb of God for sinners slain (12)

In Leviticus: He is our High Priest

In Numbers: He is the Star out of Jacob (24:17)

In Deuteronomy: He is the Prophet like unto Moses (18:15)

In Joshua: He is the Captain of the Lord's hosts (5:13–15)

In Judges: He is the Messenger of Jehovah (3:15–30)

In Ruth: He is our Kinsman-Redeemer (3)

In Samuel: He is the despised and rejected King (1 Sam. 16–19)

In Kings and Chronicles: He is the Lord of lords and King of kings (1 Chron. 12:38–40)

In Ezra and Nehemiah: He is the Lord of heaven and earth

In Esther: He is our Mordecai (10)

In Job: He is our risen and returning Redeemer (19:25)

In Psalms:

    He is the blessed Man of Psalm 1

    He is the Son of God of Psalm 2

    He is the Son of man of Psalm 8

    He is the crucified one of Psalm 22

    He is the risen one of Psalm 23

    He is the coming one of Psalm 24

He is the reigning one of Psalm 72

He is the Leader of praise of Psalm 150

In Proverbs: He is our wisdom (4)

In Ecclesiastes: He is the forgotten wise Man (9:14–15)

In Song of Solomon: He is my Beloved (2:16)

In Isaiah: He is our suffering Substitute (53)

In Jeremiah: He is the Lord our righteousness (23:6)

In Lamentations: He is the Man of sorrows (1:12–18)

In Ezekiel: He is the one sitting on the throne (1:26)

In Daniel: He is the smiting stone (2:34)

In Hosea: He is David's greater King (3:5)

In Joel: He is the Lord of bounty (2:18–19)

In Amos: He is the Rescuer of Israel (3:12)

In Obadiah: He is the Deliverer upon Mount Zion (17)

In Jonah: He is the buried and risen Savior

In Micah: He is the everlasting God (5:2)

In Nahum: He is our stronghold in the day of wrath (1:7)

In Habakkuk: He is the anchor of our faith (2:4)

In Zephaniah: He is in the midst for judgment and cleansing (3:5, 15)

In Haggai: He is the Lord of presence and power (1:13)

In Zechariah: He is the smitten Shepherd (13:7)

In Malachi: He is the sun of righteousness (4:2)

In Matthew: He is the King of the Jews (2:1)

In Mark: He is the Servant of Jehovah

In Luke: He is the perfect Son of man (3:38; 4:1–13)

In John: He is the Son of God (1:1)

In Acts: He is the ascended Lord (1:8–9)

In Romans: He is our righteousness (3:22)

In 1 Corinthians: He is the firstfruits from among the dead (15:20)

In 2 Corinthians: He is made sin for us (5:21)

In Galatians: He is the end of the law (3:10; 3:13)

In Ephesians: He is our armor (6:11–18)

In Philippians: He is the Supplier of every need (4:19)

In Colossians: He is the preeminent one (1:18)

In 1 Thessalonians: He is our returning Lord (4:15–18)

In 2 Thessalonians: He is the world's returning Judge (1:7–9)

In 1 Timothy: He is the Mediator (2:5)

In 2 Timothy: He is the Bestower of crowns (4:8)

In Titus: He is our great God and Savior (2:13)

In Philemon: He is the Father's Partner (17–19)

In Hebrews: He is the rest of faith and Fulfiller of types (9; 11; 12:1–2)

In James: He is the Lord of Sabaoth; hosts; almighty (5:4)

In 1 Peter: He is the theme of Old Testament prophecy (1:10–11)

In 2 Peter: He is the longsuffering Savior (3:9)

In 1 John: He is the Word of life (1:1)

In 2 John: He is the target of the Antichrist (7)

In 3 John: He is the personification of truth (3, 4)

In Jude: He is the believer's security (24, 25)

In Revelation: He is King of kings and Lord of lords (19:11–16)

b. GRACE

1. That which gives or yields joy, pleasure, delight, charm, sweetness, and loveliness.
2. Good will, loving kindness, mercy.
3. The kindness of a master toward a slave (i.e., the kindness of God to man—Luke 1:30).
4. The concept of kindness bestowed upon someone undeserving, or undeserved favor, especially that kind or degree of favor bestowed

upon sinners through Jesus Christ. "By God, who is rich in mercy, because of his great love with which he loved us, even when we were dead in trespasses made us alive together with Christ, by grace you have been saved" (Eph. 2:4–5).

5. Grace is the medium or instrument through which God has affected the salvation of all believers. "For the grace of God that brings salvation has appeared to all men" (Titus 2:11).

6. Grace also sustains and secures the believer enabling them to persevere (Acts 11:23, 20:32; 2 Cor. 9:14).

7. It is also a proof of our salvation, that God's grace and comfort are realities (2 Cor. 1:5).

c. SIGNIFICANCE

How can we be effective as Christians in a world that has gone crazy?

11 points to ponder!

1. Look outside yourself and circumstances for a moment. There is more in the world than this—much more (1 Cor. 2:9).

2. Why did God breathe into man, causing humans to have a soul? Why did God create you and your neighbor? Answer: Love—an exercise of God's free will. To love means to share (Eph. 1:4–6).

3. *Pros* (with) God. The Word was with God (John 1:1). *Pros* is the Greek word meaning "with." *Pros* means face-to-face, complete union, or intercourse with God. From eternity past, God the Son, God the Father, and God the Holy Spirit were in union—until the cross. "My God, My God, why hast thou forsaken me?" (Matt. 27:46) This was the first and only time in all eternity that God the Father broke fellowship with God the Son. Why? Because sin separates us fellowship with God (Isa. 59:2). Jesus became sin, paying the penalty for sin, thus breaking fellowship with the Father so that those who would trust in the shed blood of Christ could have fellowship with the Father through the Son (2 Cor. 5:20, 21). Jesus broke fellowship, becoming sin so that we might have fellowship with God. Amazing!

4. You have purpose; your neighbor has purpose (Eph. 2:10).

5. You have always been in God's mind. This is a mystery (Eph. 1:4).
6. You have been given a certain number of days on earth (Ps. 90:12).
7. God created. He is still creating. He is not finished creating you (Esther 4:14; Jer. 1:5–10).
8. You have worth; your neighbor has worth (Gen. 1:26).
9. If Christians can understand this, we would understand that each person has significance from conception until death (Gen. 2:7).
10. As a result, we would do everything in our power to tell the message of God's love to the world (Acts 1:8).
11. We would live differently; we would talk differently; we would go out of our safe, sub-cultural boxes and embrace humanity with the love of Christ, communicating in practical ways as well as profound ways. We would be different; we would be effective (Micah 6:8; Luke 14:23).

d. LONGING

"When these things were accomplished . . . there arose a great commotion about the Way . . ."

—ACTS 19:21, 23

When things are accomplished in our lives for the Lord Jesus, when changes take place for the better, be prepared for Satan's attack. When the Holy Spirit causes us to repent from sin, we must realize that the Evil One will do whatever he can to discourage and dissuade you from continuing your growth pattern.

If you long for new life and power in your Christian walk, you should do the following in God's strength:

1. Yield to the Holy Spirit's promptings. Surrender daily to him.
2. Confess specific sins. Name them. Materialism? Sensuality? Idolatry? Pride? Lying? Bitterness? Coldness of heart?

3. Ask God to give you the strength to turn back to him. Tell him you can truly repent only by his enabling grace.
4. Do whatever he tells you to do in his precious Word.
5. Rest in him.

May you be victorious today, tomorrow and in the days to come. One day, you will enjoy eternal triumph in Heaven with Christ forever. Until that day, cling to him and rest in his power and love.

e. THE WONDER OF HIS NAME

God's name reveals a different aspect of his personality, love, and provision. He is the Word who is mighty and strong, who shepherds his children, and one who sanctifies, heals, and leads; he is more than enough, as he is our righteousness and provision. Below are a few of his names.

1. The Word (John 1:1-4, 14; Proverbs 18:10)
2. Elohim (Genesis 1:1; Psalm 139)

    El—Mighty or strong, total power; mighty
    Him—Plural (Father, Son, Holy Spirit)

3. Jehovah-Rohi (Psalm 23; John 10:11)

    Jehovah is my Shepherd.

4. Jehovah-M'Kaddesh (Exodus 31:13; 1 Thessalonians 4:3)

    Jehovah who sanctifies.

5. Jehovah-Rapha (Exodus 15:26; Matthew 8:16–17)

    I am the Lord that heals you.

6. Jehovah-Nissi (Exodus 17:12–13, 15; John 12:32)

    The Lord is our banner.

7. El Shaddai (Ephesians 3:20)

    The One who is more than enough.

8. Jehovah-Tsidkenu (Jeremiah 23:5–6; 2 Corinthians 5:21)

    Jehovah our Righteousness.

9. Jehovah-Jireh (Genesis 22:13–14; John 1:29)

    The Lord will provide.

6

Questions for the Pastor

a. WHERE WILL WE DWELL IN ETERNITY?

The name "New Jerusalem" is found twice in Scripture (Rev. 3:12, 21:2). Some believe that the New Jerusalem will be inhabited by the Church, the people of God.

John was told that he would be shown the Bride, the Lamb's wife, in Revelation 21:9, and he was shown the city—the New Jerusalem, according to 21:10–11.

This city was not only given a name—the New Jerusalem—but it also possesses walls with gates that are guarded by angels and which only the redeemed can enter. Its foundation is made of precious stones and jewels. All of its citizens are saved. It is 1,500 miles square. Its glory is profound.

"Let not your heart be troubled: ye believe in God, believe also in me. In my Father's house are many mansions: if it were not so, I would have told you. I go to prepare a place for you. And if I go and prepare a place for you, I will come again, and receive you unto myself; that where I am, there ye may be also" (John 14:1–3, KJV).

However, others also believe that the inhabitants would include the Old Testament saints according to Hebrews 11:8–16 (KJV).

"By faith Abraham obeyed when he was called to go out to the place . . . for he waited for the city which has foundations, whose builder and maker is God . . . these all died in faith, not having received the promises, but having seen them afar off were assured of them, embraced them and confessed that they were strangers and pilgrims on the earth . . . . Therefore God is not ashamed to be called their God, for He has prepared a city for them."

The New Heaven and New Earth are a reference to a perfected state of the universe and that final dwelling place of the righteous.

The idea of a New Heaven and New Earth runs deep in the vein of the Jewish soul. Since the fall of man in Genesis 3, the anticipation of Messiah coming and putting things in proper order is woven through the fabric of Old Testament thought.

God promised Abraham's seed that they would inherit the land for a "thousand generations." If a generation is 30 years, we are speaking about 30,000 years. This will not happen unless there is a New Earth in which they can dwell (Deut. 7:9; 1 Chron. 16:15; Psalm 105:8; Isa. 65:17, 66:22). Therefore, it is believed that the New Earth will be for Israel.

However, it is written that the "[e]ye hath not seen, nor ear heard, neither have entered into the heart of man, the things which God hath prepared for them that love him. But God hath revealed them unto us by his Spirit: for the Spirit searcheth all things, yea, the deep things of God" (1 Cor. 2:9–10, KJV).

Though the New Jerusalem may be for the Church and the New Earth for Israel, we will inhabit, rule with, and participate in all that God has for us. James states that we are "a kind of first fruits of His creatures" (Jas. 1:18, KJV). If we are the "first fruits," then what must the whole harvest be like?

We read, "Of the increase of His government and peace there shall be no end" (Isa. 9:7, KJV). This means that his government is limitless. Paul said it this way: "Now when all things are made subject to Him, then the Son Himself will also be subject to him (God) who put all things under him, that God may be all in all" (1 Cor. 15:28, KJV). God is all in all, just as Jesus is "all in all" (Col. 3:11), for they are equal.

The idea is that God has a plan so vast, so beyond anything we could ever imagine, that one day all the universe—with its galaxies, solar systems, planets, stars, all that is realized and unrealized—will yield to the authority of Christ and the redeemed. This is known as the Great Abdication.

Paul said in Romans 8:19 and 21, "For the earnest expectation of the creation eagerly waits for the revealing of the sons of God . . . because the creation itself also will be delivered from the bondage of corruption into the glorious liberty of the children of God."

The curse will be removed and creation will be delivered. This will take place in two stages. The first stage will be during the Millennial Reign of Christ and the second with the New Heaven, New Earth, a New Jerusalem.

Oh, what a glorious day that will be when all of creation will finally be brought into harmony with Christ, when time as we know it will end and eternity begins! The "age to come" has no end, and those who believe in Christ will be there.

b. RESURRECTION OF THE OLD TESTAMENT SAINTS

There are two main views on this topic:

- A. That some Old Testament saints have already been raised, such as Moses and Elijah in Matthew 17:3, Lazarus along with others recorded for us in the New Testament, and those who rose from the grave when Christ died and rose again as recorded in Matthew 27:52–53.

There is some confusion concerning those resurrections recorded for us, such as Lazarus or Jairus' daughter (Luke 8:52–56) and whether or not they had to experience death again or if they were raised with glorified bodies like the Lord's. We just don't know.

Nevertheless, the first view is that the rest of the Old Testament saints will be raised with the Church, the Body of Christ, or the Body of Messiah, when he comes in the air at the Rapture (1 Cor. 15:52; 1 Thess. 4:14–18).

The conviction is that just as the soul who looks back to Calvary and believes that Jesus is the Christ is made part of the Body of Christ, so it was with those in the Old Testament, the ones who looked forward to the Messiah, believing that he would come, who were made part of the body of Messiah. Therefore, they will be raised at the Rapture of the Body of Christ, the Church.

- B. The second view is that the Old Testament saints will be raised at the end of the Tribulation period as part of the first resurrection, that all the saved or all the righteous will take part of the "first resurrection" (Rev. 20:5–6). The "second resurrection," concerning the wicked, is found in Revelation 20:11–15.

The first resurrection is by stages:
1. Christ being the "firstfruits" (1 Cor. 15:23).
2. Those few raised at the resurrection of Christ (Mat. 27:52–53).

3. Those raptured with the church, both dead and living, since Pentecost (Rev. 4:1; 1 Thes. 4:13–18).

4. The two witnesses resurrected and raptured during the Tribulation (Rev. 11:3, 11–12).

5. Finally, the resurrection of the martyred Tribulation saints, which would include the Old Testament saints (Rev. 20:4–6; Isa. 26:19–21; Eze. 37:12–14; Dan. 12:2–3).

This is the traditional Dispensational position held by most dispensationalists.

c. WHERE WILL THE BABY OR CHILD GO AFTER DEATH?

First of all, the Bible does not speak directly on this issue. Some suggest this may be on purpose in order not to give cultists a license for infanticide to guarantee their children's salvation. On one hand, babies and children are not ensured of heaven because of "sinlessness" or "innocence." All have sinned, even babies.

David stated, "Behold, I was shapen in iniquity, and in sin did my mother conceive me" (Psalm 51:5, KJV).

Paul said it this way: "Wherefore, as by one man sin entered into the world and death by sin; and so death passed upon all men, for that all have sinned" (Romans 5:12, KJV).

"For all have sinned" (Romans 3:23, KJV) means that because Adam sinned we all have sinned, even babies. So, a baby needs salvation, just as an adult. On the other hand, the Lord's death on the cross delivers us from sin.

In the Old Testament, particularly in the Book of Leviticus, you have offerings that typify Messiah's sacrifice for sin. For example, the "sin offering" (Leviticus 4), known also as the "guilt offering," gives us the understanding that Jesus' death guarantees deliverance from our fallen nature, from sins intentional or unintentional.

The "trespass offering" (Leviticus 5) declares that the Messiah's death on the cross provides forgiveness for every evil thought, word, and deed we commit against him. We are accountable for our sins, and yet, by God's grace through the shed blood of our Lord, we find mercy and forgiveness.

Therefore, a baby would receive forgiveness on the basis of the sin offering. Christ, the last Adam, shed his blood for us, removing the penalty for all sins, unintentional or intentional. However, when a child becomes accountable, knowing right from wrong, understanding what sin is and why Jesus died for our sins, he or she needs to be saved. This means they are now accountable and need to receive or reject the gospel.

Let's explore this further. David implied that a baby would depart to be with God. When his child died, we read these words: "While the child was yet alive, I fasted and wept: for I said, who can tell whether God will be gracious to me, that the child may live? But now he is dead, wherefore should I fast? Can I bring him back again? I shall go to him, but he shall not return to me. And David comforted Bathsheba his wife" (2 Sam. 12:22–24, KJV).

You see, David knew that there was existence after death. David believed in God and knew that he would see his child again. The implication is clear: Jesus said, "Suffer (permit) little children, and forbid them not, to come unto me: for of such is the kingdom of heaven" (Matt. 19:14, KJV). This does not directly address the issue of where a baby goes when they die; however, the passage gives us an insight to the compassion of our Lord accepting the children into his bosom.

In the final analysis, all have a sin nature, even babies, because of Adam's sin. Christ, the second Adam, became sin for us on the cross. Babies and young children unknowingly partake of the curse of the first Adam. Therefore, they unknowingly partake of the redemption of the second Adam, meaning that when a baby or a very young child dies, they are saved through the shed blood of our Lord Jesus. Jesus, our sin offering, took away the guilt and condemnation of sin. It is not until that child comes to an age of accountability, knowing right and wrong, sin and non-sin, that he or she would need to make a personal decision, accepting or rejecting Jesus as their Messiah and Savior.

I pray that this brings comfort and blessing. Praise be to God for his mercy, love, and grace through Jesus our beloved Savior!

www.ingramcontent.com/pod-product-compliance
Lightning Source LLC
Chambersburg PA
CBHW050846160426
43192CB00011B/2167